THE INSTITUTE OF INTERNATIONAL LAW'S RESOLUTION ON THE EQUALITY OF PARTIES BEFORE INTERNATIONAL INVESTMENT TRIBUNALS

The Institute of International Law's 2019 Resolution on the Equality of Parties before International Investment Tribunals represents a major step forward in codification of this essential principle as it applies to investor-state dispute settlement: a principle whose application in this context has attracted increasing controversy in recent years. In this commentary, Campbell McLachlan, who served as the Institute's Rapporteur on the topic, explains the context for the Resolution and sets forth an article-by-article analysis of its provisions, drawing upon a wealth of prior case-law as well as the discussions within the Institute that led to the Resolution. The resulting text is designed to assist counsel and tribunals in investment cases, as well as contribute to the wider debate on the reform of investor-state dispute settlement.

CAMPBELL MCLACHLAN QC is Professor of Law at Victoria University of Wellington and Arthur Goodhart Visiting Professor of Legal Science Elect in the University of Cambridge. He served as Rapporteur for the Institute of International Law's work on the Equality of Parties before International Investment Tribunals. He is Joint Editor-in-Chief of *ICSID Review – Foreign Investment Law Journal* and co-author of *International Investment Arbitration: Substantive Principles* (2nd edn, 2017). He regularly sits as an arbitrator in disputes under the aegis of the Permanent Court of Arbitration and the International Centre for the Settlement of Investment Disputes. He will give the General Course at The Hague Academy of International Law in 2024.

THE INSTITUTE OF INTERNATIONAL LAW'S RESOLUTION ON THE EQUALITY OF PARTIES BEFORE INTERNATIONAL INVESTMENT TRIBUNALS

Introduction, Text and Commentaries

CAMPBELL MCLACHLAN
Victoria University of Wellington

CAMBRIDGE
UNIVERSITY PRESS

CAMBRIDGE
UNIVERSITY PRESS

University Printing House, Cambridge CB2 8BS, United Kingdom

One Liberty Plaza, 20th Floor, New York, NY 10006, USA

477 Williamstown Road, Port Melbourne, VIC 3207, Australia

314–321, 3rd Floor, Plot 3, Splendor Forum, Jasola District Centre, New Delhi – 110025, India

103 Penang Road, #05–06/07, Visioncrest Commercial, Singapore 238467

Cambridge University Press is part of the University of Cambridge.

It furthers the University's mission by disseminating knowledge in the pursuit of education, learning, and research at the highest international levels of excellence.

www.cambridge.org
Information on this title: www.cambridge.org/9781316517826
DOI: 10.1017/9781009047586

First published 2022

Printed in the United Kingdom by TJ Books Limited, Padstow Cornwall

A catalogue record for this publication is available from the British Library.

Library of Congress Cataloging-in-Publication Data
Names: McLachlan, Campbell, author.
Title: The Institute of International Law's resolution on the equality of parties before international investment tribunals : introduction, text and commentaries / Campbell McLachlan, Victoria University of Wellington.
Description: Cambridge, United Kingdom ; New York, NY : Cambridge University Press, 2021.
Includes bibliographical references and index.
Identifiers: LCCN 2021026881 (print) | LCCN 2021026882 (ebook) | ISBN 9781316517826 (hardback) | ISBN 9781009047586 (ebook)
Subjects: LCSH: Institute of International Law. Equality of parties before international investment tribunals. | Investments, Foreign (International law) | International commercial arbitration. | Equality before the law.
Classification: LCC K3830 .M389 2021 (print) | LCC K3830 (ebook) | DDC 346/.092–dc23
LC record available at https://lccn.loc.gov/2021026881
LC ebook record available at https://lccn.loc.gov/2021026882

ISBN 978-1-316-51782-6 Hardback

CONTENTS

PREFACE

The heavy responsibility of being appointed, immediately upon election to the *Institut de Droit International*, as Rapporteur of its Eighteenth Commission on the 'Equality of Parties before International Investment Tribunals' was greatly alleviated by the enthusiastic support of the members of the Commission.[1] Their detailed insights and willingness to work together to find a compromise solution enabled the Commission to present a consensus draft resolution to the plenary session of the *Institut* in The Hague in August 2019. The *Institut* adopted the resolution by large majority during that session.[2]

The Resolution aims to contribute to the current debate, both within arbitral institutions and under the aegis of UNCITRAL Working Group III, on the reform of investor–State arbitration, through its consideration of the implications of the equality principle for the design of international investment tribunals, whether arbitral or permanent. It also aims to provide practical guidance of enduring utility to parties, their counsel and tribunal members in the resolution of the many issues of procedure and evidence that engage equality considerations during the course of a dispute.

These factors suggested that a detailed commentary on the resolution, in the manner of the commentaries on International Law Commission draft articles, would assist users of the resolution. Fortunately, Marcelo Kohen, Secretary-General of the *Institut*, had already established an excellent precedent, with his commentaries (with Patrick Dumberry) on the *Institut*'s resolution on State succession and State responsibility.[3] With his kind encouragement, I have attempted to provide similar guidance on the equality resolution.

I wish to thank in particular the New Zealand Law Foundation, a grant from which supported the research, and Eve Bain, who provided excellent research assistance throughout.

Campbell McLachlan
Wellington, New Zealand
August 2021

1 Stanimir Alexandrov, Laurence Boisson de Chazournes, James Crawford, Pierre d'Argent, Giorgio Gaja, Andrea Giardina, Sir Christopher Greenwood, Mojtaba Kazazi, Marcelo Kohen, Vaclav Mikulka, August Reinisch, Brigitte Stern, Tullio Treves, P S Rao and Raul Vinuesa.

2 The Report and Preparatory Works are at (2019) 79 *Annuaire* 409–618. The debate in plenary is at (2019) 80 *Annuaire* 1–70.

3 Kohen and Dumberry 2019.

TABLE OF CASES

ABBREVIATIONS

AC	Appeal Cases
A-G	Attorney-General
AJIL	American Journal of International Law
ALI	American Law Institute
Am U Int'l LR	American University International Law Review
Annals AAPSS	Annals of the American Academy of Political and Social Science
Arb Int'l	Arbitration International
ASEAN	Association of Southeast Asian Nations
BCDR Int'l Arb Rev	BCDR International Arbitration Review
BIT	bilateral investment treaty
CETA	Canada–EU Comprehensive Economic and Trade Agreement
CIDS	Center for International Dispute Settlement
CIETAC	China International Economic and Trade Arbitration Commission
CJEU	Court of Justice of the European Union
CMLR	Common Market Law Review
CPTPP	Comprehensive and Progressive Trans-Pacific Partnership Agreement
Czech YBIL	Czech Yearbook of International Law
DSU	Dispute Settlement Understanding
EC	European Commission
ECHR	European Convention on Human Rights
ECommHR	European Commission on Human Rights
ECT	Energy Charter Treaty
ECtHR	European Court of Human Rights
EFILA	European Federation for Investment Law and Arbitration
EHRR	European Human Rights Reports
EU	European Union
Eur Rev	European Review
FTC	Free Trade Commission
German LJ	German Law Journal
IACtHR	Inter-American Court of Human Rights

IBA	International Bar Association
ICC	International Chamber of Commerce
ICCA	International Council for Commercial Arbitration
ICCPR	International Covenant on Civil and Political Rights
ICJ	International Court of Justice
ICJ Rep	ICJ Reports
ICLQ	International Comparative Law Quarterly
ICSID	International Centre for the Settlement of Investment Disputes
ICSID Rep	ICSID Reports
ICSID Rev – FILJ	ICSID Review – Foreign Investment Law Journal
IFAD	International Fund for Agricultural Development
ILA	International Law Association
ILC	International Law Commission
ILM	International Legal Materials
ILO	International Labour Organization
ILOAT	ILO Administrative Tribunal
Indian LR	Indian Law Review
ISDS	Investor–State Dispute Settlement
IUSCT	Iran–US Claims Tribunal
JIDS	Journal of International Dispute Settlement
JIEL	Journal of International Economic Law
J Int'l Arb	Journal of International Arbitration
JWIT	Journal of World Investment & Trade
LCIA	London Court of International Arbitration
LPICT	Law and Practice of International Courts and Tribunals
Max Planck UNYB	Max Planck Yearbook of United Nations Law
Mich JIL	Michigan Journal of International Law
NAFTA	North Atlantic Free Trade Agreement
OJ	Official Journal of the European Union
PCA	Permanent Court of Arbitration
PCIJ	Permanent Court of International Justice
PCIJ Rep	PCIJ Reports
SIAC	Singapore International Arbitration Centre
Texas LR	Texas Law Review
TRIMS	Agreement on Trade-Related Investment Measures
TTIP	Transatlantic Trade and Investment Partnership Agreement
UDHR	Universal Declaration of Human Rights
UKSC	UK Supreme Court
UKTS	UK Treaty Series
UN	United Nations

UNAT	UN Administrative Tribunal
UNCITRAL	UN Commission on International Trade Law
UNCLOS	UN Convention on the Law of the Sea
UNCTAD	UN Conference on Trade and Development
UNESCO	UN Educational, Scientific, and Cultural Organization
UNGA Res	UN General Assembly Resolution
UNHRC	UN Human Rights Committee
UNTS	UN Treaty Series
VCLT	Vienna Convention on the Law of Treaties
WTO	World Trade Organization
YB Comm Arb	Yearbook of Commercial Arbitration
YB ILC	Yearbook of the International Law Commission

I
INTRODUCTION

A Equality as a Constitutional and a Procedural Principle

The equality of the parties is a fundamental element of a fair system of adjudication, whether within a national legal system or at international law. The International Court of Justice has observed that: 'The principle of equality of the parties follows from the requirements of good administration of justice.'[1] 1

One of the objectives that States sought to achieve through their development of international investment arbitration by treaty was 'the transformation of a relationship from one of disequilibrium … to equilibrium'.[2] Investment arbitration aims to do this by placing disputes between two parties of a different and asymmetrical character – a private investor and a State – before an international arbitral tribunal before whom each party is in principle to be treated equally. 2

The fundamental character of the equality principle in investment arbitration was recognised from the outset of the development of the ICSID Convention.[3] In one of the earliest decisions to construe the scope of annulment of an award for 'a serious departure from a fundamental rule of procedure', an *ad hoc* Committee stated: 'a clear example of such a fundamental rule is to be found in Article 18 of the UNCITRAL Model Law on International Commercial Arbitration which provides: "The parties shall be treated with equality and each party shall be given full opportunity of presenting his case."'[4] 3

Yet, as the International Court has also had cause to observe, the concept of equality in its actual application to the procedure of courts and tribunals has developed over time.[5] 4

Experience with investment arbitration, especially over the last two decades in which it has been most actively utilised, has given rise to debate as to the application of the equality 5

1 *Judgments of the Administrative Tribunal of the ILO upon complaints made against UNESCO* (Advisory Opinion) [1956] ICJ Rep 77, 86.

2 Franck 1993: 452.

3 Convention on the Settlement of Investment Disputes between States and Nationals of Other States ('ICSID Convention') (signed 18 March 1965, entered into force 14 October 1966) 575 UNTS 159. On this point, see ICSID 1969: II, 480 (Broches).

4 *Maritime International Nominees Establishment (MINE) v Guinea* (Decision on Annulment) ICSID Case No ARB/84/4 (1989) 4 ICSID Rep 87 (Sucharitkul P, Broches & Mbaye), [5.06].

5 *Judgment No 2867 of the Administrative Tribunal of the International Labour Organization ('ILOAT') upon a Complaint filed against the International Fund for Agricultural Development ('IFAD')* (Advisory Opinion) ('*Judgment No 2867*') [2012] ICJ Rep 10, [39].

principle in this distinctive form of international dispute resolution. The debate has engaged at two levels: *procedural* and *constitutional.*

6 *At a procedural level*, arbitral tribunals and institutions have had to consider the implications of the equality of the parties for jurisdiction and admissibility of claims and counterclaims; as well as for the production of evidence and the protection of the arbitral process from abusive conduct. These issues have arisen in the practice of arbitral decision-making. They form part of a larger enquiry into the fundamental elements of the procedure of international courts and tribunals.[6]

7 *At the constitutional level*, there has been an increasing controversy over whether arbitration is in fact the most appropriate forum for the resolution of investment disputes. A debate among scholars and in civil society has led to a number of initiatives to examine different dispute settlement mechanisms. Most notable among these is the European Commission proposal for an Investment Court, with a standing Tribunal and Appeal Tribunal – a proposal that has already resulted in the inclusion of such arrangements in the text of two free trade agreements.[7] At its Fiftieth Session in July 2017, and following a preparatory study prepared by the Geneva Center for International Dispute Settlement (CIDS),[8] UNCITRAL decided to include 'Reforms of investor–State dispute settlement' on its future work programme.[9] The CIDS Report is an important scientific contribution to the current debate, which addresses the legal issues that would arise in the design of an International Tribunal for Investments in the event that States were to decide to pursue the establishment of such a Tribunal.

8 On 20 March 2018, the Council of the European Union endorsed the European Commission's proposal to create a Multilateral Investment Court and conferred a negotiating mandate upon the Commission.[10] These negotiations are taking place in the first instance through UNCITRAL Working Group III (Investor–State Dispute Settlement Reform).[11] Within its broad mandate to work on the possible reform of investor–State dispute settlement, the Working Group has given consideration to the establishment of a multilateral advisory centre, development of a code of conduct for arbitrators, third-party funding, appellate and multilateral court mechanisms, as well as selection and appointment of tribunal members.[12] The Working Group has a number of further reform options on its agenda, including security for costs, means to address frivolous claims and multiple proceedings (including counterclaims).[13] In the course of the policy debate, one of the

[6] Kotuby and Sobota 2017; Sarvarian et al 2015.

[7] Art 8.27, Canada–EU Comprehensive Economic and Trade Agreement (CETA) (signed 30 October 2016, entered into force provisionally 21 September 2017); Ch 3, arts 3.38–3.57, Final Text of EU–Vietnam Investment Protection Agreement (signed 30 June 2019, entered into force 1 August 2020), http://trade.ec.europa.eu/doclib/press/index.cfm?id=1437.

[8] Geneva CIDS (Kaufmann-Kohler and Potestà) 2016.

[9] UNCITRAL 2017a, UN Doc A/CN.9/917.

[10] EU Council 2018.

[11] Ibid, [4]; UNCITRAL 2018, UN Doc A/CN.9/935. For an analysis of States' preliminary positions, see Roberts 2018.

[12] UNCITRAL 2020a, UN Doc A/CN.9/1004/Add.1.

[13] UNCITRAL 2019a, UN Doc A/CN.9/1004.

criticisms of investment arbitration that has been made concerns whether *constitutionally* arbitration is capable of offering a fair and balanced method for the resolution of international investment disputes.[14] Other prominent scholars argue that investment arbitration does provide a fair system for the resolution of investment disputes and should not be abandoned or replaced, precisely because it offers the best means of balancing the interests of both parties.[15]

B The Contribution of the *Institut*

The *Institut* has considered issues of arbitral procedure in both public and private international law since its foundation. It considered the general aspects of arbitral procedure in public international law at its session in The Hague in 1875, returning to this subject in Lausanne in 1927. It addressed arbitration in private international law at its Amsterdam session in 1957 and dealt with more specific aspects of arbitral settlement of disputes in 1999[16] and 2003.[17] **9**

The previous contributions of the Eighteenth Commission. The Eighteenth Commission has previously dealt with arbitration between States and foreign investors in two phases of its work: **10**

(1) Between 1984 and 1989, the Commission (Rapporteurs E Jiménez de Arechaga and R von Mehren) addressed the topic of 'Arbitration and Foreign Enterprises'.
(2) Between 2009 and 2013, the Commission (Rapporteur A Giardina) took up legal aspects of recourse to arbitration by an investor against the authorities of the host State under inter-State treaties.

In each case, the research of the Commission resulted in a resolution that was adopted by the *Institut* after debate in plenary session. These resolutions provide both the background to the present work of the Commission and contribute some relevant elements to the issue. **11**

Arbitration between States and foreign enterprises. The *Institut* adopted a resolution on 'Arbitration between States, state enterprises, or state entities and foreign enterprises' at its Santiago de Compostela session in 1989.[18] At that stage, the Eighteenth Commission's work and the resulting resolution were primarily concerned with arbitrations pursuant to **12**

14 See, e.g., Al-Khasawneh 2015: ix, xiii–xv; 'An Open Letter about Investor–State Dispute Settlement' (20 April 2015), www.osgoode.yorku.ca/public-statement-international-investment-regime-31-august-2010; Malmström 2017.

15 See, e.g., 'An Open Letter'; Bernadini 2017; EFILA 2015; Schwebel 2016. On the issues generally, see Bonnitcha et al 2017: ch 9.

16 'Judicial and Arbitral Settlement of International Disputes involving more than two States' (Berlin, 1999).

17 'Arbitral settlement of international disputes other than between States involving more than two parties' (Bruges, 2003).

18 (1989) 63 *Annuaire* Pt I, 31–204 (preparatory work), Pt II, 121–2 (deliberations of the Institut), 324–31 (Resolution as adopted).

specific contractual agreements between States and foreign enterprises. The Rapporteurs considered that treaty-based arbitrations raised quite different problems,[19] the Preamble '*[n]oting* that this Resolution is without prejudice to the applicable provisions of international treaties'.[20]

13 The preparation of that report and resolution occasioned an extended debate in the *Institut* about the specific issues arising in arbitrations between States and foreign enterprises. In its Resolution, the *Institut* accepted that the issues arising in such arbitrations are 'a subject of great practical as well as theoretical importance' and require a 'statement of a coherent body of principle regarding the arbitrator's role and obligations in such arbitrations [which] will clarify certain fundamental questions and contribute to legal security.'[21]

14 Its operative provisions lay primary emphasis upon the parties' agreement for arbitration as the basis for the arbitrators' authority and powers (art 1). It seeks to uphold such agreements 'guided in every case by the principle *in favorem validitatis*' (art 4), and specifically excluding objections to the tribunal's jurisdiction based upon a State's incapacity to arbitrate (art 5) or sovereign status (art 9). It emphasises the autonomy of the parties to choose the applicable procedural as well as substantive rules, enjoining the tribunal in the absence of such choice to supply the necessary rules and principles, choosing from a wide array of potential legal sources (art 6).

15 The *Institut* did not regard the parties' autonomy to control the procedure as unlimited. Article 1 imposes a duty on the arbitrator to 'exercise his functions impartially and independently'. Article 2 adds: 'In no case shall an arbitrator violate principles of international public policy as to which a broad consensus has emerged in the international community.' A working draft introduced by the Rapporteurs in the course of the plenary session would have specifically referred in this context to 'the principles of due process'.[22] Although this express statement did not survive in the final text, this was not because members expressed any doubt that due process is a principle of international public policy. Rather, the plenary decided that it did not wish to limit the principles of international public policy to procedural matters. It rather wished to embrace a more capacious conception of international public policy to include substantive policies.[23]

16 *Investment treaty arbitration.* More recently, the Eighteenth Commission (Rapporteur A Giardina) addressed a broad range of topics of current importance concerning legal aspects of recourse to arbitration by an investor against the authorities of the host State under inter-state treaties, following a general outline of work adopted at the Naples session in 2009. This work culminated in a resolution adopted at Tokyo in 2013 on 'Legal aspects

19 (1989) 63 *Annuaire* Pt I, 43–4.
20 Emphasis in the original.
21 Preamble (1989) 63 *Annuaire* II, 324.
22 (1989) 63 *Annuaire* II, 160.
23 Ibid, 173 (Lalive), 174 (concurring views), 180 (Goldman revised text), 182 (vote).

of recourse to arbitration by an investor against the authorities of the host State under inter-state treaties'.[24]

This resolution endorses 'the need to ensure a balanced protection of the interests of the involved parties'. It deals with general and substantive law issues. Apart from the matters dealt with under 'General Issues', this resolution does not cover procedural issues.[25] The Commission decided to exclude procedural topics, since otherwise it would not have been possible for it to complete its mandate. In the preamble to the resolution, the *Institut* reserved such 'more specific matters for further discussion' on the basis that 'certain recurring problems call for the elaboration of principles enjoying wide support'. **17**

In summary, prior to its work on equality that is the subject of the present resolution, the *Institut* had recognised that party autonomy in arbitrations between States and foreign enterprises is subject to the limits imposed by international public policy, which concept it considered undoubtedly includes the requirements of due process. It had not given detailed consideration to what might be the content of procedural principles of international public policy. It has reserved matters of procedure within the context of investment treaty arbitration for subsequent consideration in its search for principles enjoying wide support. It is against this background that a reconstituted Eighteenth Commission was invited in 2015 by the *Commission des travaux* to study the application of the principle of the equality of parties before international investment tribunals. **18**

The present work of the Eighteenth Commission on equality. The Commission consisted of: M Alexandrov, Mme Boisson de Chazournes, MM. Crawford, d'Argent, Gaja, Giardina, Greenwood, Kazazi, Kohen, Mikulka, Reinisch, Mme Stern, MM. Treves, Rao and Vinuesa. It first met in Hyderabad on Sunday 3 September 2017 – the occasion of the 78th Session of the *Institut*. **19**

The Members of the Commission had before them a detailed *rapport préliminaire* prepared by the Rapporteur and circulated to them on 20 August 2017, which provided background research on the issues. **20**

The Rapporteur had also included in that report a questionnaire to members on the issues of law and legal policy arising from his research on the issues, as to which he sought the guidance of the Commission's members. Members furnished full responses to the questionnaire.[26] These responses revealed a large measure of consensus among Commission members on many of the issues raised. **21**

In light of members' responses, the Rapporteur revised the *rapport préliminaire* and circulated members in October 2018 with a draft of the *rapport provisoire*, which also included reference to a number of material contributions to State practice, doctrine and **22**

[24] (2013) 75 *Annuaire* 1; Giardina (2014) 29 ICSID Rev – FILJ 701.

[25] Giardina (2014) 29 ICSID Rev – FILJ 709, 710.

[26] (2019) 79 *Annuaire* 543–91.

jurisprudence in the year to 30 September 2018. At the same time, he prepared a draft *avant-projet* for a resolution that might be presented to the plenary.

23 The report and draft resolution were revised in light of the comments of members of the Commission.

24 The resolution was tabled for debate and adoption at the 79th Session of the *Institut* held at the Peace Palace, The Hague on 27 and 28 August 2019.[27] It was adopted by the *Institut* by a large majority on 28 August 2019.[28]

C Scope of the Resolution

25 The topic as framed by the *Institut's Commission des travaux* links two elements. The *subject* of study is the equality of parties as a procedural principle. Its *object* is the forum constituted by international investment tribunals. Some preliminary elucidation of each element is required.

26 In the first place, the present Resolution is limited to the application of the principle of the equality of the parties in the *process* by which international investment disputes are resolved. It will not examine the substantive principles enshrined in investment treaties.[29]

27 In the second place, the object of study refers generally to 'international investment tribunals'. This expression is apt to include both arbitral tribunals and standing international tribunals with competence in the investment field. The latter category could include both extant tribunals, such as the Iran–US Claims Tribunal (which has extensive relevant practice on this topic) and those that are not yet established (such as the standing tribunals now incorporated in some EU bilateral treaties or the proposed International Tribunal for Investments).[30]

28 The question of the most appropriate forum and procedures for the resolution of investment disputes raises a much wider set of issues than the equality principle. Ultimately, the question of whether a new standing tribunal is to be created is a policy question for States. Even if such a tribunal is established, it is unlikely to replace arbitration, which would continue to apply in cases not covered by any new arrangements or where States and investors agreed to resolve their dispute by arbitration instead of resorting to the standing tribunal. In any event, an elucidation by the *Institut* of the equality principle and an

27 (2019) 80 *Annuaire* 1–70.

28 81 votes in favour, 2 votes against and 7 abstentions: (2019) 80 *Annuaire* 51.

29 The substantive assurance of equality of treatment forms an important part of the standards of fair and equitable treatment, national treatment and most favoured nation treatment commonly found in investment treaties: Dolzer and Schreuer 2012: chs 18–20; McLachlan et al 2017: [7.214]–[7.223].

30 Some proposals for standing tribunals envisage in any event that they may properly be treated as a form of arbitration, whose decisions will be enforceable as awards: arts 8.23 and 8.41, CETA; Geneva CIDS (Kaufmann-Kohler and Potestà) 2016: [91]–[99].

examination of the problems that have arisen in practice in its application will assist in the progressive development of fair procedures for the resolution of international investment disputes, whether by arbitration or within a standing international tribunal.

D Equality in Asymmetrical Dispute Resolution Systems

To what extent do the particular characteristics of investment arbitration pose unique challenges in the application of the equality of the parties? Can it be said that the asymmetrical character of such arbitration, which brings a private party and a State before the same tribunal, is inherently unequal or requires special adjustments to assure equality? 29

In order to address this question, it is necessary to examine in outline first the position in the context of two related systems of international adjudication: (1) diplomatic protection and the development of claims commissions and tribunals; and (2) international human rights commissions and tribunals. It will then be possible to turn to the solutions specific to investor–State arbitration adopted in the ICSID Convention 1965. 30

Diplomatic protection and claims commissions. The contemporary system under which an individual investor may pursue his or her claim directly against a State was developed in part as a response to perceived shortcomings in the remedy of diplomatic protection that is otherwise open to the investor's home State in the event that its national suffers a wrong at the hands of the host State which constitutes a breach of international law.[31] 31

Arbitral tribunals determining diplomatic protection claims invoked the equality principle. But the nature of such a claim is that it substitutes the claim of the State for that of its national vis-à-vis the State whose international responsibility is said to have been engaged.[32] As a result, the Tribunal has before it two States Parties, each of which is the juridical equal of the other. 32

Nevertheless, international law has developed procedures enabling an individual to pursue a claim directly against a host State outside the specific context of investment arbitration. 33

Prior to World War I, there were only isolated instances of claims procedures where the direct intervention of the affected individual had been permitted.[33] The position changed in the inter-war period, where there was increasing (but not uniform) recognition that the individual might enjoy direct rights under an international treaty, including the right to seek compensation before an international tribunal from a State for breach of treaty rights.[34] For example, the Upper Silesian Mixed Commission and Arbitral Tribunal recognised that the 34

[31] Broches 1972: 344. See also Polanco 2019.

[32] Art 1, International Law Commission, Draft Articles on Diplomatic Protection [2006] 2(2) YB ILC 23.

[33] Parlett 2011: ch 2.

[34] Ibid, 71–7.

individual had, pursuant to the treaties establishing them, full procedural capacity to pursue his or her claims against a State.[35]

35 The most salient example of a standing tribunal with jurisdiction to determine individual claims against a State created in the post-World War II period is the Iran–US Claims Tribunal, which has consistently rejected the suggestion that it is determining diplomatic protection claims or inter-State disputes and insisted that it is a new forum in which individual claimants vindicate their own rights.[36] As the Tribunal adopted (in modified form) the UNCITRAL Arbitration Rules, its decisions form an important source of jurisprudence on the interpretation and application of the equality principle.[37]

36 The Tribunal has particularly had cause to invoke the equality principle in its character as the *principe de la contradiction*, or right of each party to respond to the submissions of its opponent:

> Article 15 of the Tribunal Rules requires that the Tribunal treat the parties equally. This is a fundamental principle of justice. In the circumstances of these cases, the delicate balance of equality would be tipped if one party were to be permitted to present an extensive Memorial and additional exhibits, without providing an opportunity for the other party to file a memorial in response.[38]

37 The important point for present purposes is that the ability of individual claimants to assert claims before the Tribunal has not proved to be fundamentally inconsistent with an assurance of equality of the parties.

38 The international legal system has also accommodated an asymmetrical form of adjudication in the field of human rights.[39] Both the Inter-American and the European systems admit a right of individual petition against State action as 'a key component of the machinery for protecting the rights and freedoms set forth in the Convention'.[40] In the Inter-American system,[41] and originally in the European system, this application had first to be made to a Commission.

39 In the case of the European Convention, the right of individual petition to the Commission was originally dependent upon the State Party making a declaration that it accepted this right.[42] In 1990, the Committee of Ministers adopted Protocol No 9, which provided for

35 Kaeckenbeeck 1946.
36 *Esphahanian v Bank Tejarat* (1983) 2 Iran–US CTR 157, 165.
37 See Caron and Caplan 2013.
38 *Foremost Tehran Inc v Iran* (1983) 3 Iran–US CTR 361, 362.
39 Lixinski 2015: ch 18.
40 *Mamatkulov v Turkey*, Nos 46827/99 and 46951/99 (Merits and Just Satisfaction) [2005] ECHR 64, (2005) 41 EHRR 25 (6 February 2003), [122]; art 34, ECHR.
41 Arts 44 and 61, American Convention on Human Rights (signed 22 November 1969, entered into force 18 July 1978) 1144 UNTS 123.
42 Schabas 2015: 735.

direct individual access to the Court. One of the reasons advanced for this amendment was that limiting access to the Court to the Commission and to States Parties, and excluding a right of direct individual petition, was incompatible with the norms enshrined in the Convention, being a denial of equality of arms.[43] Ultimately, by Protocol No 11, which entered into force in 1998,[44] the Commission was abolished and the right of individual direct access to the Court was enshrined in Article 34 of the Convention as revised.

In interpreting Article 34, the Court has held that bodies exercising public functions are not entitled to bring an individual application 'as a person, non-governmental organisation or group of individuals claiming to be the victim of a violation by one of the High Contracting Parties of the rights set forth in the Convention'. The Court explained that 'the idea behind this principle is to prevent a Contracting Party acting as both an applicant and a respondent party before the Court'.[45] The key distinction is not whether the applicant is publicly owned, but whether the body exercises public functions or is instead independent from the State.[46] **40**

As a result, the right of individual petition is designed as an asymmetrical system for the adjudication of the claims of private individuals against the State. Although the Convention contained from the outset Article 33, which entitles States to enforce the provisions of the Convention *erga omnes partes*, in practice that procedure has long been eclipsed in practical significance by the volume of individual complaints.[47] **41**

In deciding individual complaints, the human rights tribunals accept that they must themselves accord procedural equality. In the Inter-American system, the Court considered the compliance of the Inter-American Commission with due process requirements in an advisory opinion. It held: 'The processing of individual petitions is regulated by guarantees that ensure each party the exercise of the right of defense in the proceedings. These guarantees [include] . . . procedural equality.'[48] **42**

E The ICSID Convention

The ICSID Convention 1965, currently ratified by 155 States,[49] constitutes a unique, self-contained system for the arbitration of investment disputes between 'Contracting States and nationals of other Contracting States'.[50] Although investment disputes may also be **43**

43 Explanatory Report on Protocol No 9, [12], cited in Schabas 2015: 28.
44 Protocol No 11, ETS 155.
45 *Islamic Republic of Iran Shipping Lines v Turkey*, No 40998/98 [2007] V ECHR 327, [81].
46 *The Holy Monasteries v Greece* (Admissibility and Merits) (ECtHR, 1994) Ser A No 301-A, (1995) 20 EHRR 1, [49].
47 Schabas 2015: 723–30.
48 *Control of Legality in the Practice of Authorities of the Inter-American Commission of Human Rights* (Advisory Opinion) OC-19/05 IACtHR (28 November 2005) Ser A No 19, [27].
49 ICSID, 'Database of ICSID Member States', https://icsid.worldbank.org/en/Pages/about/Database-of-Member-States.aspx.
50 Preamble recital 4, ICSID Convention.

arbitrated *ad hoc* or under the auspices of other arbitration institutions,[51] the special character and wide ratification of the ICSID Convention as a dispute resolution system mean that its own treatment of the equality principle is of particular importance to the present study.

44 The Convention does not mention the equality principle expressly. Nevertheless, the equality of the parties was an important guiding principle in its framing. Aron Broches, General Counsel to the World Bank and the driving force behind the creation of the Convention, identified one of its most distinctive features as being the creation of facilities for arbitration 'to which the host country and the foreign investors would be parties on an equal procedural footing'.[52] The Executive Directors emphasised that, 'since the Convention permits the institution of proceedings by host States as well as by investors', they 'have constantly had in mind that the provisions of the Convention should be equally adapted to the requirements of both cases'.[53]

45 The requirement on tribunals to observe equality of the parties as a procedural matter is a fundamental rule of ICSID arbitral procedure. It is given effect in the structure of the arbitral procedure contemplated by the ICSID Convention and implemented by the Arbitration Rules. Its content has been elaborated in particular in the decisions of *ad hoc* annulment committees charged with determining whether 'there has been a serious departure from a fundamental rule of procedure'.[54]

46 By its current Proposals for Amendment of the ICSID Rules, the Secretariat proposes to make explicit that which was previously implicit by adding a new Rule 11(1), which states: 'The Tribunal shall treat the parties equally and provide each party with a reasonable opportunity to present its case.'[55] The accompanying Working Paper for the first version of the Proposed Rules explains that this addition is confirmatory and adopts wording similar to Article 17(1) of the UNCITRAL Rules 2010.[56]

47 The framers of the ICSID Convention ensured the application of the equality principle by providing that one ground for the annulment of an award is 'that there has been a serious departure from a fundamental rule of procedure'.[57] This provision adopts the language of the International Law Commission (ILC) Model Rules.[58] The *travaux préparatoires* indicate that the fundamental rules of procedure that the drafters had in mind were to be restricted to the principles of natural justice, including that both parties must be heard with adequate opportunity for rebuttal.[59]

51 For the division between ICSID and non-ICSID cases, see UNCTAD 2020.
52 Broches 1972: 344.
53 ICSID 1965: [13].
54 Art 52(1)(d), ICSID Convention.
55 ICSID 2020b: vol 1, 125.
56 ICSID 2018a: [108].
57 Art 52(1)(d), ICSID Convention.
58 Art 35(c), International Law Commission, Model Rules on Arbitral Procedure [1958] 2 YB ILC 83; Schreuer et al 2009: 898.
59 ICSID 1969: II, 480.

Early decisions on the interpretation of this provision confirmed that equality of treatment of the parties and the impartiality of the arbitral tribunal vis-à-vis the parties are such fundamental rules.[60] As the Annulment Committee in *Wena Hotels* put it, this provision **48**

> ... refers to a set of minimum standards of procedure to be respected as a matter of international law. It is fundamental, as a matter of procedure, that each party is given the right to be heard before an independent and impartial tribunal. This includes the right to state its claim or its defence and to produce all arguments and evidence in support of it. This fundamental right has to be ensured on an equal level, in a way that allows each party to respond adequately to the arguments and evidence presented by the other ...[61]

The central importance of the equality of the parties in the conception of 'a fundamental rule of procedure' was emphasised by the Annulment Committee in *Fraport*.[62] The Committee considered submissions as to three principles, each of which was said to be a fundamental rule of procedure. The first two, *nullum crimen sine lege* and *in dubio pro reo*, were alleged by the claimant to have been violated by the Arbitral Tribunal when it construed a host State statute in its consideration of whether the investment had been admitted in accordance with host State law. The third was the right to be heard where the Tribunal had permitted one party to adduce additional documentary evidence after the hearing, without giving the other party the opportunity to comment on it. **49**

The Committee rejected the submission that the first two principles were to be treated as fundamental rules of procedure for the purpose of the ICSID Convention, but accepted the third. The essential ground of distinction in its analysis was an application of the equality principle. **50**

It held that the *nullum crimen* principle is a fundamental human rights principle in the context of criminal law, but that 'it would be a distortion of the important function of the principle to consider it applicable in the present context as a fundamental rule of procedure'.[63] It found that it was not procedural in character, but applies to the determination of the scope of the substantive law. **51**

The Committee rejected the application of the principle *in dubio pro reo* on the ground that: **52**

> [S]uch a principle cannot be applied in the context of international arbitral proceedings instituted by an investor against a state. *Indeed, the application of*

[60] *Maritime International Nominees Establishment (MINE) v Guinea* (Decision on Annulment) ICSID Case No ARB/84/4 (1989) 4 ICSID Rep 87 (Sucharitkul P, Broches & Mbaye), [5.06]; *Amco Asia Corporation v Indonesia* (Decision on Annulment) ICSID Case No ARB/81/1 (1986) 1 ICSID Rep 509 (Seidl-Hohenveldern P, Feliciano & Giardina), [88].

[61] *Wena Hotels Ltd v Egypt* (Decision on Annulment) ICSID Case No ARB/98/4 (2002) 6 ICSID Rep 129 (Kerameus P, Bucher & Orrego Vicuña), [57].

[62] *Fraport AG Frankfurt Airport Services Worldwide v The Philippines* (Decision on Annulment) ICSID Case No ARB/03/25 (2010, Tomka P, Hascher & McLachlan).

[63] Ibid, [191].

> *such a presumption could itself, in the context of ICSID proceedings, amount to a failure of due process since it may unbalance the essential equality between the parties.* The principle *in dubio* has proper application as a right of the defence in criminal proceedings, because it counterbalances the coercive power of the state. It cannot, however, be transposed into the context of international arbitral proceedings, because to do so would be inconsistent with the principle of equality of the parties.[64]

53 By contrast, the right to be heard on additional evidence is, in the view of the Committee, a part of the right to present one's case, which is 'an essential element of the requirement to afford a fair hearing'.[65] This 'requires both equality of arms and the proper participation of the contending parties in the procedure, these being separate but related fundamental elements of a fair trial'.

54 In light of these introductory remarks, it is now possible to examine in more detail, in Part II, the text of the Resolution as adopted in the two working languages of the Institute – English and French – and, in Part III, to analyse its provisions by way of commentary.

64 Ibid, [193] (emphasis added).
65 Ibid, [202].

II
TEXT

This chapter sets out the final text of the Resolution, as adopted by the Institute at its 79th Session in The Hague on 31 August 2020 in each of the Institute's working languages, English[1] and French.[2] **55**

A Final English Text of the Resolution (August 2019)

The English text is as follows: **56**

Eighteenth Commission

Equality of Parties before International Investment Tribunals
Rapporteur: Mr Campbell McLachlan

Resolution

The Institute of International Law,

Considering that the principle of equality of the parties is a fundamental element of the rule of law that ensures a fair system of adjudication and as such is a general principle of law applicable to the procedure of international courts and tribunals, as reflected in their jurisprudence.

Observing that the equality of the parties is also a fundamental human right recognised by Article 10 of the Universal Declaration of Human Rights of 1948 and Article 14(1) of the International Covenant on Civil and Political Rights of 1966,

Recalling that the Eighteenth Commission, in its Report to the Tokyo Session in 2013, had reserved for further consideration the principles applicable to the procedure of investment arbitration,

Acknowledging the contribution made by the United Nations Commission on International Trade Law ('UNCITRAL') and by the International Bar Association

[1] (2019) 80 *Annuaire* 62.
[2] (2019) 80 *Annuaire* 54.

('IBA') to the elaboration of important aspects of the principle of equality of the parties in its application to international arbitration generally,

Mindful that the Convention on the Settlement of Investment Disputes between States and Nationals of Other States of 1965 ('ICSID Convention') provides a framework for the resolution of investment disputes that has to date been widely adopted by States and that the International Centre for the Settlement of Investment Disputes ('ICSID') is currently conducting a review of its Rules of Procedure for Arbitration Proceedings ('ICSID Arbitration Rules'),

Recognising that States resolved at the Fiftieth Session of UNCITRAL in 2017 to take up the topic of reform of investor–State dispute settlement, including consideration of the possibility of the establishment of a permanent International Tribunal for Investments, and that the application of the principle of the equality of the parties is one of the matters under consideration in that context,

Resolving that the application of the equality principle requires specific consideration in light of the particular characteristics of international investment disputes, in which the tribunal has before it two parties of a different juridical character: a private investor and a State, whose function it is to represent the public interest,

Determining that its consideration of this question should consider the position of both kinds of arbitral tribunals, whether are appointed *ad hoc* to decide a particular case ('arbitral tribunal') or any standing tribunal that is constituted now or in the future to decide investment disputes ('permanent tribunal'),

Adopts the following Resolution:

Part One Application to the Establishment of the Tribunal

CHAPTER 1 FORUM

ARTICLE 1
Legal character

(1) The extent to which a dispute between the national of one State ('the investor') and another State ('the State') in respect of an investment may be submitted to the jurisdiction of an international investment tribunal ('the tribunal') results from the scope of the parties' consent. Submission of such a dispute to the tribunal engages the principle of the equality of the parties.
(2) Such a forum is designed to secure equality between the parties in circumstances where the State has the sovereign power to enforce its own law and adjudicate its claims against investors for breach of its laws before its own courts.

ARTICLE 2
Access

(1) Both the State and the investor are equally entitled to submit a claim in relation to an investment to a tribunal, subject to the terms of the instrument of consent, interpreted in accordance with the principle of the equality of the parties.
(2) No State is obliged to submit its claim against an investor to a tribunal, unless it gives its consent and elects to do so. Otherwise, a State remains entitled to use the rights and remedies provided by its own national legal system in order to pursue such a claim before its own courts.
(3) The limitation of access to the investor of another State bears a direct relationship to the object of investment treaties, which is to promote and protect foreign investment and the rights of foreign nationals, while also respecting the State's sovereign right to regulate investment activities within its jurisdiction in the public interest. It does not infringe the principle of equality of access. Such protection is equally available to the investors of each State when they make an investment within the scope of the treaty protections by investing in the territory of the other State.

CHAPTER 2 TRIBUNAL

ARTICLE 3
Impartiality

(1) The impartiality of all members of a tribunal is an indispensable prerequisite to the equality of the parties.
(2) The substantive standards applicable to the determination of any question relating to the impartiality of a member of an arbitral tribunal should be uniform and transparent.

(3) The IBA Guidelines on Conflicts of Interest in International Arbitration 2014 provide a useful framework of substantive rules within which to analyse questions that may arise as to the impartiality of a member of an arbitral tribunal constituted to decide an investment dispute.
(4) Challenges to the impartiality of a member of an arbitral tribunal should be determined by an independent third party decision-maker external to the tribunal.
(5) As a consequence States parties to the ICSID Convention are encouraged to amend Article 58 so as to refer the determination of challenge applications to an independent third party decision-maker in all cases.

ARTICLE 4

Composition

(1) The composition of a tribunal shall be determined through a process of appointment that ensures that the parties to any dispute heard by that tribunal are treated with equality.
(2) This is so whether the tribunal is constituted as an arbitral tribunal or is established as a permanent tribunal. The composition of both kinds of tribunal must respect the equality of the parties; but the different legal character of arbitration and a permanent judicial body dictate a different application of the principle in each case:

   (a) The resolution of investment disputes by an arbitral tribunal composed of members appointed equally by the parties, with the president appointed by agreement (or, failing agreement, designated by an appointing authority) respects the principle of the equality of the parties, provided also that each member meets the same requirements of impartiality.
   (b) In the case of a permanent tribunal, the principle of the equality of the parties does not require that each party retain the ability to appoint a judge. The overriding consideration is the independence and impartiality of the members of the tribunal.

(3) A permanent tribunal of universal scope should comprise a body of independent judges of recognized competence in international law that equitably represents the principal legal systems of the world, elected through a transparent process.
(4) In the resolution of a specific dispute within the framework of a permanent tribunal, in order to respect the equality principle the rules governing the composition of a Bench or Chamber should either:

   (a) Exclude judges having the nationality of either the State party to the dispute or of the home State of the foreign investor; *or*,
   (b) Ensure that both such States have an equal opportunity to appoint a judge, if necessary by making provision for the appointment of a judge *ad hoc*.

Part Two Application to the Procedure of the Tribunal

CHAPTER I PARTIES

ARTICLE 5

Multiple claimants

(1) Where several investors seek to institute their claims in a single arbitral proceeding against the same State, the tribunal shall ensure, in its determination of jurisdiction and admissibility and in its procedural directions, that the parties are treated with equality.

(2) When determining its jurisdiction, the tribunal must be satisfied that:

(a) Each claimant individually satisfies the jurisdictional requirements (both of the instrument of consent and, where applicable, Article 25 of the ICSID Convention) in order to bring its claim; and

(b) The claim as a whole advances a single dispute, in that the interest represented by the claimants is in all respects identical, so that the respondent is not prejudiced by having to defend itself against claims that differ materially in the interest to be vindicated.

The tribunal may hold a claim brought by multiple claimants to be inadmissible if it finds that the manner in which the claim is brought would adversely affect the tribunal's ability to ensure that both sides of the dispute are treated with equality in the presentation of their case or in their defence of the claims.

ARTICLE 6

Counterclaims

(1) The ability of a respondent to assert a counterclaim that is admissible before a tribunal ensures the procedural equality of the parties.

(2) In order to be admissible, such a counterclaim must:

(a) Be within the jurisdiction of the tribunal; and,

(b) Arise directly out of the subject matter of the investment.

(3) The jurisdictional requirement is met when, by virtue of the instrument of consent invoked by the respondent, the tribunal would have had jurisdiction over the counterclaim had it been asserted as a primary claim. Whether or not the tribunal has jurisdiction over a counterclaim does not depend upon the respondent invoking the same ground of jurisdiction as that relied upon by the claimant for its claim, nor is the tribunal's jurisdiction limited by the scope of the dispute as framed by the claimant in its Request for Arbitration.

(4) Where the dispute is submitted to arbitration under the ICSID Convention, the requirement in Article 46 that the counterclaim must also be 'otherwise within the

jurisdiction of the Centre' means that it must fall within the criteria of Article 25(1) of the Convention by being a 'legal dispute arising directly out of an investment, between a Contracting State . . . and a national of another Contracting State.'

(5) The requirement of sufficiency of connection with the subject matter of the dispute is met where the counterclaim concerns the same investment that gave rise to the claim. It does not require that the counterclaim be founded upon the same legal instrument or cause of action asserted by the claimant.

(6) The tribunal may find a counterclaim to be admissible, whether it is founded upon international law or host State law, provided that it fulfils the other requirements set out in this Article and concerns a subject matter that is capable of submission to arbitration.

ARTICLE 7

Third person submissions

(1) Third person submissions may valuably assist a tribunal to determine the dispute, where they bring a perspective, knowledge or insight that is different from that of the disputing parties.

(2) In order to protect the equality of the parties, in accordance with the UNCITRAL Rules on Transparency in Treaty-based Investor–State Arbitration 2014:

- (a) The third person shall disclose any connection, direct or indirect, which it has with either of the disputing parties, their counsel or members of the tribunal or the subject-matter of the dispute;
- (b) The tribunal shall ensure that the disputing parties are given a reasonable opportunity to present their observations on any third person submission; and,
- (c) The tribunal shall ensure that any such submission does not unfairly prejudice either disputing party.

CHAPTER 2 PLEADING AND EVIDENCE

ARTICLE 8

Equality of arms

(1) The equality of the parties includes the principle of the equality of arms, namely that:

- (a) Each party shall have the right to be heard on the submissions of the other (*audi alteram partem*); and,
- (b) Each party shall enjoy reciprocal treatment in the procedural timetable and in matters of pleading, production of documents and evidence.

(2) The tribunal should order and enforce a procedural timetable, which promotes both efficiency and equality of the parties.

(3) Where, exceptionally, a party is able to establish a compelling case for the admission of late evidence or pleading, the tribunal must be satisfied that, if it admits the evidence or pleading, it is able to afford the other party equality of treatment, including an effective right to be heard on the new material.

(4) Equality of treatment in a hearing requires that each party be allocated substantial equality of time to plead and present its evidence; subject always to the tribunal's overall authority to ensure the fair and efficient conduct of the hearing, taking into account the number of witnesses and its own mandate to hear and test the evidence and arguments of the parties.

ARTICLE 9

Production of Documents and Evidence

(1) During the written phase, each party shall produce to the other the evidence on which it relies, so that the other party has a reasonable opportunity to respond.

(2) The same standards shall be applied to adjudge the requests of both parties for the production of specific documents. The IBA Rules on the Taking of Evidence in International Arbitration 2010 provide a useful general framework for such determinations.

(3) In ordering a timetable for production, the tribunal should take into account the particular challenges faced by States, especially developing States, in locating and producing documents. This must be balanced against ensuring that the other party has an adequate opportunity to consider and respond to the documents within the procedural timetable.

(4) Where the investor is part of a group of companies, the principles of equality and good faith require that it should use best efforts to produce relevant documents that are held by its parent or affiliated companies or shareholders, when the respondent State so requests and the tribunal so directs.

(5) Where a party has requested the attendance of a witness for cross-examination at the hearing and the party relying on the evidence of that witness fails without a valid reason to produce that witness, the tribunal may (save in exceptional circumstances) disregard that evidence in order to preserve the procedural equilibrium between the parties.

ARTICLE 10

Objections to production

(1) The tribunal shall apply the equality principle in making decisions with regard to pleas of privilege from disclosure, in light of the fact that the applicable standards may differ between the national laws of the parties. The tribunal should strive to apply a standard that operates equally for both parties.

(2) Where the parties raise objections to disclosure with regard to documents on grounds of, respectively, commercial confidentiality or State secrecy, the tribunal should

strive to secure a balance of treatment between the parties so as to ensure that each party has the ability to obtain evidence that is relevant and material to the issues in dispute, whilst at the same time respecting the wider interests of each party beyond the instant case and relevant policy considerations.

(3) In the case of a plea of State secrecy, the tribunal shall balance the public interest in the administration of justice which supports disclosure against the public interest underlying the confidentiality of governmental communications.

(4) In so doing, it should invite the parties to agree protocols for the protection of confidentiality or secrecy in documents or parts thereof applicable in the case before the tribunal.

(5) In a case in which an objection to production is raised:

(a) The objection must be justified with sufficient specificity in order to enable the opposing party to contest it and the objection to be determined;
(b) The tribunal has discretion whether to accept the objection, balancing the public interests involved;
(c) The tribunal shall apply international law to its decision on the objection;
(d) The tribunal should, in appropriate cases, consider, in consultation with the parties, appointing an independent third party expert to review the documents and decide contested objections to production.

ARTICLE 11

Improper means

(1) Both parties owe a duty to each other and to the tribunal to conduct themselves in the proceedings in good faith.

(2) The tribunal has the power to exclude evidence where it is satisfied that it has been obtained in violation of the principle of good faith and that it is essential to do so in order to preserve the equality of the parties.

(3) Exceptionally, in order to protect the fairness of its own procedure and the equality of the parties, the tribunal may recommend to the State measures concerning the effect of the exercise of its powers of criminal investigation and prosecution upon the tribunal's own process.

(4) In such a case, the tribunal will only act on the basis of clear evidence of conduct that is aimed at obtaining an unfair advantage in the proceedings before it or otherwise imperils the fair conduct of those proceedings.

CHAPTER 3 SUBSTANTIVE EQUALITY OF ARMS

ARTICLE 12

Costs

(1) The ability of parties, whether investors or States, to pursue or defend claims before a tribunal should not be determined on grounds of cost. Particular regard should be

paid in this context to the position of small and medium-sized enterprises and to that of developing States.

(2) Where a party's pursuit of its claim or defence is supported by third party funding, that party shall disclose the identity of the third party funder, so that the tribunal may consider, inter alia, any possible implications for the maintenance of the impartiality of the tribunal.

(3) Where on application the tribunal is satisfied that a claimant may be unable to pay an award of costs in the event that its claim is unsuccessful and that the provision of security is necessary to preserve the equal protection of the parties, the tribunal has discretion to order security for costs.

B Final French Text of the Resolution (August 2019)

57 The French text is as follows:

18ème Commission

L'égalité des parties devant les tribunaux internationaux d'investissements

Rapporteur: M. McLachlan

Resolution

L'Institut de Droit international,

Considérant que le principe d'égalité des parties est un élément fondamental de l'état de droit qui garantit un règlement juridictionnel juste et, à ce titre, constitue un principe général de droit de la procédure des cours et tribunaux internationaux, tel qu'il résulte de leur jurisprudence,

Constatant que l'égalité des parties est aussi un droit humain fondamental reconnu à l'article 10 de la Déclaration universelle des droits de l'homme de 1948 et à l'article 14(1) du Pacte international relatif aux droit civils et politiques de 1966,

Rappelant que la 18ème Commission, dans son rapport à la Session de Tokyo de 2013, avait renvoyé le sujet des principes applicables à la procédure en matière d'arbitrage d'investissements à un examen ultérieur,

Reconnaissant la contribution faite par la Commission des Nations Unies pour le droit commercial international (CNUDCI), et par l'*International Bar Association* (IBA) à l'élaboration d'importants aspects du principe d'égalité des parties dans son application en matière d'arbitrage international en général,

Conscient que la Convention internationale pour le règlement des différends relatifs aux investissements entre Etats et ressortissants d'autres Etats de 1965 (Convention CIRDI) fournit un cadre pour la résolution des différends en matière d'investissements qui a, à ce jour, été adopté par de nombreux Etats et que le Centre international pour le règlement des différends relatifs aux investissements (CIRDI) révise actuellement son Règlement de procédure relatif aux instances d'arbitrage (Règlement d'arbitrage CIRDI),

Notant que les Etats ont décidé, lors de la cinquantième session de la CNUDCI en 2017, de se saisir du sujet de la réforme du règlement des différends investisseur-Etat, y compris la possibilité de créer un tribunal international permanent pour les investissements, et que l'application du principe d'égalité des parties est une des questions examinées dans ce contexte,

Estimant que l'application du principe d'égalité requiert un examen spécifique au vu des caractéristiques particulières des différends en matière d'investissements internationaux, lesquels opposent deux parties de nature juridique distincte : un investisseur privé et un Etat, le rôle de ce dernier étant de représenter l'intérêt public,

Déterminant que son examen de la question devra s'intéresser aux deux types de tribunaux arbitraux, qu'ils soient institués de manière *ad hoc* pour trancher un litige précis (tribunal arbitral) ou qu'il s'agisse de tribunaux permanents déjà constitués ou qui pourraient l'être dans l'avenir en vue de trancher des différends relatifs aux investissements (tribunal permanent),

Adopte la résolution suivante :

Première Partie Application du Principe d'Egalité à la Création du Tribunal

CHAPITRE I LE FOR

ARTICLE 1ER

Caractère juridique

1. La mesure dans laquelle un différend entre le ressortissant d'un Etat (« l'investisseur ») et un autre Etat (« l'État ») au sujet d'un investissement peut être soumis à la compétence d'un tribunal international d'investissement (« le tribunal ») dépend de l'étendue du consentement des parties. La soumission de ce différend au tribunal implique l'application du principe d'égalité des parties.
2. Un tel for vise à garantir l'égalité des parties dans une situation où l'État peut souverainement faire appliquer son propre droit et soumettre à ses propres juridictions les différends qui l'opposent à des investisseurs pour violation de sa législation.

ARTICLE 2

Accès au tribunal

1. Sous réserve des termes de l'acte exprimant leur consentement interprété conformément au principe d'égalité des parties, l'État et l'investisseur sont tous deux fondés à intenter devant un tribunal une action se rapportant à un investissement.
2. À moins d'y consentir et de le choisir, aucun Etat n'est tenu d'intenter une action à un investisseur devant un tribunal. S'il ne l'a pas fait, l'État reste fondé à faire usage des droits et recours prévus par son ordre juridique national en vue de faire valoir ses droits devant ses propres juridictions.
3. Les limites posées à l'accès au tribunal pour un investisseur d'un autre Etat sont directement liées à l'objet même des traités d'investissement, lesquels visent à promouvoir et protéger les investissements étrangers et les droits des ressortissants étrangers, tout en respectant le droit souverain de l'État à règlementer, dans l'intérêt public, les activités d'investissement sur son territoire. Ces limites ne doivent pas

porter atteinte au principe d'égalité. Une telle protection est accessible sur un pied d'égalité aux investisseurs de chaque Etat lorsqu'ils font un investissement couvert par le traité dans l'autre Etat.

CHAPITRE II LE TRIBUNAL

ARTICLE 3
Impartialité

1. L'impartialité de tous les membres du tribunal est un prérequis indispensable à l'égalité des parties.
2. Les standards matériels applicables à la décision sur toute question relative à l'impartialité d'un membre du tribunal arbitral devraient être uniformes et transparents.
3. Les Lignes directrices sur les conflits d'intérêts en arbitrage international adoptées par l'IBA en 2014 fournissent un cadre utile de règles matérielles pour analyser les questions qui peuvent être soulevées quant à l'impartialité d'un membre du tribunal arbitral constitué pour trancher un litige d'investissement.
4. Toute contestation visant l'impartialité d'un membre du tribunal arbitral devrait être examinée par une instance tierce indépendante extérieure au tribunal.
5. Dès lors, les Etats parties à la Convention CIRDI sont invités à amender l'article 58 de façon que l'examen des demandes en récusation soit confié, dans tous les cas, à une instance tierce indépendante extérieure au tribunal.

ARTICLE 4
Composition du tribunal

1. La composition du tribunal doit résulter d'un processus de désignation assurant une égalité de traitement aux parties à tout différend soumis à ce tribunal.
2. Il en est ainsi que le tribunal soit constitué comme tribunal arbitral ou comme tribunal permanent. La composition de ces deux types de tribunaux doit respecter l'égalité des parties ; néanmoins, la différence de nature juridique entre l'arbitrage et un organe juridictionnel permanent requiert une application différenciée du principe d'égalité, adaptée à chaque cas :

   a) Le règlement des différends d'investissement par un tribunal arbitral composé de membres nommés à part égale par les parties et, pour le président, par accord entre elles (ou désigné, en l'absence d'accord, par une autorité investie du pouvoir de nomination) respecte le principe d'égalité des parties, pourvu que chaque membre du tribunal satisfasse aux mêmes conditions d'impartialité.
   b) Dans le cas d'un tribunal permanent, le principe d'égalité des parties n'exige pas que chaque partie conserve la capacité de nommer un juge. Priorité absolue est donnée à l'indépendance et à l'impartialité des membres du tribunal.

3. Un tribunal permanent de caractère universel devrait être composé d'un corps de juges indépendants dont la compétence en droit international est reconnue et qui, dans son

ensemble, représente équitablement les principaux systèmes juridiques du monde, et qui sont élus selon un processus transparent.

4. Afin de respecter le principe d'égalité dans le cadre du règlement d'un différend spécifique par un tribunal permanent, les règles relatives à la composition de ce tribunal ou de la chambre devraient :

   a) exclure tout juge ayant la nationalité de l'État partie au différend ou de l'État d'origine de l'investisseur étranger ; ou,
   b) assurer que chacun des deux Etats en cause puisse nommer un juge, si nécessaire un juge *ad hoc*.

Deuxième partie Application du Principe d'Egalité à la Procedure du Tribunal

CHAPITRE I PARTIES

ARTICLE 5

Demandeurs multiples

1. Si plusieurs investisseurs cherchent à intenter une action dans le cadre d'une procédure arbitrale unique contre le même Etat, le tribunal s'assure, lors de l'examen de sa compétence et de la recevabilité des demandes, ainsi que lors de l'adoption des directives procédurales, que les parties sont traitées sur un pied d'égalité.
2. En déterminant sa compétence, le tribunal doit s'assurer que :

   a) chaque demandeur satisfait aux critères de compétence (de l'acte exprimant le consentement à l'arbitrage et, le cas échéant, de l'article 25 de la Convention CIRDI) lui permettant de présenter sa demande; et que,
   b) la demande dans son ensemble constitue un différend unique, en ce que les intérêts représentés par les demandeurs sont à tous égards identiques, de sorte que le défendeur ne soit pas lésé du fait de devoir se défendre contre des demandes qui représentent des intérêts matériellement différents.

3. Le tribunal peut déclarer irrecevable une demande introduite par plusieurs demandeurs s'il estime que la manière dont la demande a été introduite est susceptible d'avoir une incidence négative sur sa capacité à assurer un traitement égal des parties quant à la présentation ou la défense de leurs prétentions respectives.

ARTICLE 6

Demandes reconventionnelles

1. La capacité du défendeur de présenter une demande reconventionnelle recevable devant un tribunal garantit l'égalité procédurale des parties.
2. Afin d'être déclarée recevable, une telle demande reconventionnelle doit :

a) relever de la compétence du tribunal ; et
b) découler directement de l'objet de l'investissement.

3. La condition de la compétence est remplie lorsque, en vertu de l'acte exprimant le consentement juridictionnel invoqué par le défendeur, le tribunal aurait eu compétence pour connaître de la demande reconventionnelle si elle avait été introduite à titre principal. La compétence pour connaître d'une demande reconventionnelle ne dépend pas du fait que le défendeur s'appuie ou non sur la même base de compétence que celle sur laquelle se fonde le demandeur pour sa demande, pas plus qu'elle n'est limitée par l'étendue du différend telle que formulée par le demandeur dans sa demande d'arbitrage.
4. Lorsque le différend est soumis à l'arbitrage en vertu de la Convention CIRDI, l'exigence posée à l'article 46 selon laquelle la demande reconventionnelle doit relever « par ailleurs de la compétence du Centre » signifie qu'elle doit satisfaire au critère de l'article 25(1) de la Convention : il doit s'agir d'un différend « d'ordre juridique entre un Etat contractant . . . et le ressortissant d'un autre Etat contractant qui [est] en relation directe avec un investissement ».
5. L'exigence d'un lien suffisant avec l'objet du différend est remplie lorsque la demande reconventionnelle porte sur l'investissement qui a donné lieu à la demande. Il n'est pas nécessaire que la demande reconventionnelle soit fondé sur le même acte juridique ou la même cause que ceux invoqués par le demandeur.
6. Le tribunal peut déclarer une demande reconventionnelle recevable, qu'elle soit fondée sur le droit international ou le droit national de l'État d'accueil, pourvu qu'elle satisfasse aux autres exigences du présent article et porte sur un objet susceptible d'être soumis à l'arbitrage.

ARTICLE 7

Observations présentées par des tiers

1. Les observations présentées par des tiers peuvent utilement assister le tribunal dans son examen du différend lorsqu'elles offrent une perspective, des informations ou des éléments différents de ceux que les parties au litige ont soumis.
2. En vue de protéger l'égalité des parties, et conformément au Règlement de la CNUDCI sur la transparence dans l'arbitrage entre investisseurs et États fondé sur des traités de 2014 :

   a) le tiers doit déclarer tout lien, direct ou indirect, qu'il a avec toute partie au litige, ses conseils, les membres du tribunal ou l'objet du différend ;
   b) le tribunal doit s'assurer que les parties au litige ont une possibilité raisonnable de présenter leurs vues sur toute observation faite par un tiers ; et,
   c) le tribunal doit s'assurer qu'aucune observation du tiers ne cause de préjudice injustifié à l'une des parties au litige.

CHAPITRE II PLAIDOIRIE ET PREUVE

ARTICLE 8

Egalité des moyens

1. L'égalité des parties comprend le principe d'égalité des moyens, à savoir :

   a) chaque partie a le droit d'être entendue au sujet des conclusions de l'autre partie (*audi alteram partem*) ; et,
   b) une réciprocité de traitement doit être assurée à chaque partie s'agissant du calendrier procédural, ainsi qu'en matière de plaidoiries, de production de documents et de preuves.

2. Le tribunal devrait prescrire et faire respecter un calendrier procédural favorisant l'efficacité et l'égalité des parties.
3. Dans les cas exceptionnels où une partie présente des arguments convaincants pour faire admettre des éléments de preuve ou des pièces de procédure tardifs, le tribunal doit s'assurer, s'il fait droit à la demande, que l'autre partie sera traitée sur un pied d'égalité et, notamment, qu'elle puisse s'exprimer sur ces nouveaux éléments.
4. L'égalité de traitement lors des audiences exige que chaque partie se voie allouer une période de temps substantiellement égale pour plaider et présenter ses moyens de preuve, toujours sous réserve de l'exercice par le tribunal de son autorité en vue d'assurer une conduite équitable et efficace des audiences, compte tenu du nombre de témoins et de l'obligation qui lui incombe de prendre connaissance des moyens de preuve et des arguments des parties et de les évaluer.

ARTICLE 9

Preuve

1. Durant la phase écrite de la procédure, chaque partie présente ses moyens de preuve à l'autre de manière à offrir à cette dernière une opportunité raisonnable d'y réagir.
2. Les mêmes standards sont applicables à la décision du tribunal sur les demandes présentées par les parties en vue de la production de documents spécifiques. Les Règles sur l'administration de la preuve en arbitrage international adoptées par l'IBA en 2010 offrent un cadre utile à ce type de décision.
3. Lorsqu'il prescrit un calendrier de production de documents, le tribunal devrait tenir compte des difficultés particulières rencontrées par les Etats, notamment les Etats en développement, pour localiser et produire ces documents. Un équilibre doit être trouvé par le tribunal afin de garantir à l'autre partie une possibilité adéquate de prendre connaissance et réagir aux documents dans le cadre du calendrier procédural.
4. Lorsque l'investisseur appartient à un groupe de sociétés, les principes d'égalité et de bonne foi exigent qu'il déploie ses meilleurs efforts pour produire les documents pertinents détenus par les sociétés-mères ou affiliées ou par les actionnaires, si l'État défendeur en fait la demande et si le tribunal y fait droit.

5. Lorsqu'une partie a requis la présence d'un témoin à l'audience en vue de son contre-interrogatoire et que la partie qui s'appuie sur la preuve apportée par ce témoin omet, sans raison valable, de le présenter, le tribunal peut (sauf circonstance exceptionnelle) écarter le moyen de preuve concerné afin de préserver l'équilibre procédural entre les parties.

ARTICLE 10

Objections à la production de documents et de preuves

1. Le tribunal doit appliquer le principe d'égalité lorsqu'il statue sur des demandes de non-divulgation au titre d'information protégée, en tenant compte du fait que les standards applicables peuvent varier selon les droits nationaux des parties. Le tribunal devrait s'efforcer d'appliquer un standard qui fonctionne de manière égale pour les deux parties.
2. Lorsqu'une partie soulève des objections à la divulgation de documents en raison, respectivement, du secret des affaires ou du secret d'Etat, le tribunal devrait s'efforcer de trouver un équilibre dans le traitement des parties afin que leur capacité de se procurer des moyens de preuve qui sont pertinents et qui se rapportent aux questions litigieuses soit garantie, tout en respectant les intérêts de chaque partie qui vont au-delà du cas d'espèce ainsi que toute considération pertinente de politique générale.
3. Si un secret d'Etat est invoqué, le tribunal met en balance l'intérêt public dans l'administration de la justice, qui justifie la divulgation des documents, et l'intérêt public à préserver la confidentialité des communications gouvernementales.
4. Ce faisant, le tribunal devrait inviter les parties à conclure des protocoles visant à protéger la confidentialité ou le secret des documents, ou de parties de ceux-ci, qui portent sur le cas d'espèce.
5. Lorsqu'une objection est faite à la production d'un document :

   a) cette objection doit être motivée de manière suffisamment précise pour permettre à la partie adverse de la contester et au tribunal de statuer sur elle ;
   b) le tribunal a le pouvoir discrétionnaire d'accepter l'objection ou non en mettant en balance les intérêts publics en cause ;
   c) en statuant sur l'objection, le tribunal applique le droit international ;
   d) dans les cas qui s'y prêtent, le tribunal devrait envisager, en consultation avec les parties, la nomination d'un expert indépendant qui examine les documents et tranche les objections contestées.

ARTICLE 11

Moyens illicites

1. Au cours de la procédure, les parties ont le devoir d'agir en bonne foi l'une envers l'autre et envers le tribunal.

2. Le tribunal a le pouvoir d'exclure tout moyen de preuve si, à son jugement, ce moyen a été obtenu en violation du principe de bonne foi et si la décision est nécessaire pour préserver l'égalité entre les parties.
3. Exceptionnellement, et en vue de protéger le caractère équitable de sa propre procédure ainsi que l'égalité entre les parties, le tribunal peut recommander à l'Etat l'adoption de mesures relatives aux effets découlant de l'exercice de ses prérogatives en matière d'enquête criminelle et de poursuites concernant la procédure du tribunal.
4. Dans un tel cas, le tribunal n'agit que sur la base de la preuve claire d'un comportement visant à obtenir un avantage indu dans la procédure en cours ou nuisant à sa conduite équitable de cette procédure.

CHAPITRE III EGALITÉ MATERIELLE DES MOYENS

ARTICLE 12
Frais de procédure

1. La capacité des parties, qu'elles soient des investisseurs ou des Etats, d'intenter une action ou de défendre leurs droits devant un tribunal ne devrait pas être déterminée sur la base des frais de procédure. Dans ce contexte, il convient de porter une attention particulière à la situation des petites et moyennes entreprises ainsi qu'à celle des Etats en développement.
2. Lorsque les frais d'une action ou de la défense des droits d'une partie sont assumés par un tiers, cette partie doit en divulguer l'identité afin que le tribunal puisse examiner, notamment, toute incidence que ce financement peut avoir sur le maintien de l'impartialité du tribunal.
3. Si le tribunal estime, après examen de la demande d'une partie, que celle-ci pourrait ne pas être en mesure de s'acquitter des frais de la procédure dans l'éventualité où elle n'obtiendrait pas gain de cause, et s'il est d'avis que la constitution d'une garantie est nécessaire pour préserver l'égale protection des parties, le tribunal a le pouvoir discrétionnaire d'ordonner le cautionnement des frais de procédure.

III
COMMENTARIES

58 Chapter III provides a commentary on each of the provisions of the Resolution. It is based on the research conducted by the Rapporteur for his report, and the comments of the members of the 18th Commission.[1] It reflects the final text as adopted by the Institute in plenary, and includes references to relevant citations up to August 2020.

1 The Report and the *travaux préparatoires* of the 18th Commission are published in (2019) 79 *Annuaire* 409–618.

A Preamble

The *Institute of International Law*,

Considering that the principle of equality of the parties is a fundamental element of the rule of law that ensures a fair system of adjudication and as such is a general principle of law applicable to the procedure of international courts and tribunals, as reflected in their jurisprudence,

Observing that the equality of the parties is also a fundamental human right recognised by Article 10 of the Universal Declaration of Human Rights of 1948 and Article 14(1) of the International Covenant on Civil and Political Rights of 1966,

Recalling that the Eighteenth Commission, in its Report to the Tokyo Session in 2013, had reserved for further consideration the principles applicable to the procedure of investment arbitration,

Acknowledging the contribution made by the United Nations Commission on International Trade Law ('UNCITRAL') and by the International Bar Association ('IBA') to the elaboration of important aspects of the principle of equality of the parties in its application to international arbitration generally,

Mindful that the Convention on the Settlement of Investment Disputes between States and Nationals of Other States of 1965 ('ICSID Convention') provides a framework for the resolution of investment disputes that has to date been widely adopted by States and that the International Centre for the Settlement of Investment Disputes ('ICSID') is currently conducting a review of its Rules of Procedure for Arbitration Proceedings ('ICSID Arbitration Rules'),

Recognising that States resolved at the Fiftieth Session of UNCITRAL in 2017 to take up the topic of reform of investor–State dispute settlement, including consideration of the possibility of the establishment of a permanent International Tribunal for Investments, and that the application of the principle of the equality of the parties is one of the matters under consideration in that context,

Resolving that the application of the equality principle requires specific consideration in light of the particular characteristics of international investment disputes, in which the tribunal has before it two parties of a different juridical character: a private investor and a State, whose function it is to represent the public interest,

Determining that its consideration of this question should consider the position of both kinds of arbitral tribunals, whether are appointed *ad hoc* to decide a particular case ('arbitral tribunal') or any standing tribunal that

is constituted now or in the future to decide investment disputes ('permanent tribunal').

59 The preamble consists of eight recitals, which serve to situate the substantive principles in the Resolution in the context against which they were developed. Recitals (3)–(6) relate the present Resolution to the earlier work of the Institut and to the work of other relevant codification bodies. Recital (7) notes the premise for the present specific consideration of the application of the equality principle to investment disputes, namely the asymmetrical character of the two parties: a private investor and a State, whose function it is to represent the public interest. Recital (8) confirms a basic point of scope, namely that the Resolution is intended to apply to both arbitral and permanent tribunals. The Introduction (Chapter I) to this Commentary explains the importance of each of these elements.

60 Recitals (1) and (2) deserve more detailed consideration here. They each relate the equality of the parties to broader considerations of principle:

(1) Recital (1) considers the status of equality as a 'fundamental element of the rule of law that ensures a fair system of adjudication and as such is a general principle of law applicable to the procedure of international courts and tribunals, as reflected in their jurisprudence'.
(2) Recital (2) considers equality as a fundamental human right.

I EQUALITY IN THE JURISPRUDENCE OF INTERNATIONAL COURTS AND TRIBUNALS

61 The equality principle in investment arbitration is derived from a more general recognition of the fundamental character of ensuring the equality of the parties to a dispute in general international law.

62 The principle that a fair hearing requires equality of treatment of the parties is so closely connected with the concept of justice itself that it may be said to be inherent in the concept of a judicial or arbitral procedure. As Cheng put it: 'there are two cardinal aspects of a judicial process, the impartiality of the tribunal and its corollary, the juridical equality between the parties in their capacity as litigants'.[2]

63 The principle of equality is an integral element of the rule of law. As it was put in the UN Secretary-General's Report, *The Rule of Law at the National and International Levels*:

> The United Nations defines the rule of law as a principle of governance in which all persons, institutions and entities, public and private, including the State itself, are accountable to laws that are publicly promulgated, equally enforced and independently adjudicated, and which are consistent with

[2] Cheng 1953: 290.

> international human rights norms and standards. It requires, as well, measures to ensure adherence to the principles of supremacy of law, *equality before the law*, accountability to the law, fairness in the application of the law, separation of powers, participation in decision-making, legal certainty, avoidance of arbitrariness and procedural and legal transparency.[3]

International Court of Justice. The International Court of Justice has considered and applied the principle of the equality of the parties in a number of its decisions.[4] The principle is expressly recognised in relation to States that are not parties to the Statute, the conditions for the admission of which shall in no case 'place the parties in a position of inequality before the Court'.[5] The Court has repeatedly affirmed that 'the equality of the parties to the dispute must remain the basic principle for the Court'.[6] In the case of its contentious jurisdiction, it is **64**

> derived from the principle of the sovereign equality of States, which is one of the fundamental principles of the international legal order and is reflected in Article 2, paragraph 1 of the Charter of the United Nations. More specifically, equality of the parties must be preserved when they are involved, pursuant to Article 2, paragraph 3, of the Charter, in the process of settling an international dispute by peaceful means.[7]

The Court has referred with approval to the interpretation of the right to equality of the parties applied by the Human Rights Committee to Article 14 of the International Covenant on Civil and Political Rights 1966 (ICCPR) in its General Comment No 32 and applied considerations set out in that Comment to its own procedures.[8] **65**

The Court has had to confront the application of the equality principle, in particular, in a series of cases brought as requests by UN organs or affiliated agencies under its advisory opinion jurisdiction in relation to decisions of international administrative tribunals. The issue that the Court had to address in these cases was the inequality potentially arising from the fact that, under its Statute, only States or (in the case of advisory opinions) international organisations have standing to bring proceedings and to be heard by the Court.[9] The complainant in the underlying administrative proceedings – the officer or employee of the relevant agency – has no corresponding *locus standi*. The Court has had to seek to balance its duty to exercise the jurisdiction conferred on it by UN agencies to provide **66**

3 UN Secretary-General 2012, UN Doc A/66/749: [2] (emphasis added and internal references omitted).

4 Kolb 2013: 1119–27; Pellet 2012: [29]–[32]. The principle of equality of the parties has also been frequently invoked in Separate and Dissenting Opinions of Judges of the Court. In the interests of brevity, the present analysis is confined to Judgments and Orders of the Court.

5 Art 35(2), Statute of the International Court of Justice (signed 26 June 1945, entered into force 24 October 1945) 59 Stat 1055, UKTS 67 ('ICJ Statute').

6 *Military and Paramilitary Activities in and against Nicaragua (Nicaragua v United States of America)* (Judgment – Merits) [1986] ICJ Rep 14, [31].

7 *Seizure and Detention of Certain Documents and Data (Timor-Leste v Australia)* (Provisional Measures) [2014] ICJ Rep 147, [27].

8 *Judgment No 2867*, [39].

9 Art 34 (Competence of the Court in its contentious jurisdiction); Arts 65–6 (Advisory opinions).

advisory opinions and the limitation imposed on it by its constituent Statute with the general principle of equality.

67 In its first Opinion on this issue, delivered in 1956 under the then terms of the Statute of the ILO Administrative Tribunal (ILOAT),[10] the Court sought to distinguish the inequality of the Parties in terms of access to the Court by stating that such inequality 'does not in fact constitute an inequality before the Court. It is antecedent to the examination of the question by the Court. It does not affect the manner in which the Court undertakes that examination.'[11]

68 It nevertheless accepted that the question of equality also arises in connection with the procedure itself, since UNESCO's challenge to the result of the proceedings before the ILOAT would affect the rights of the individuals to the benefit of the judgment of that Tribunal. It recognised that '[t]he judicial character of the Court requires that both sides directly affected by these proceedings should be in a position to submit their views and their arguments to the Court'.[12] It found this requirement to be sufficiently addressed in the case before it, because UNESCO (the United Nations Educational, Scientific, and Cultural Organization) had delivered a statement on behalf of the officials to the Court and there had been no oral proceedings. In reaching this conclusion, the Court was motivated by the principle that a 'nominal absence of equality' ought not to be allowed to defeat the object of 'a régime [sic] established by the Statute of the Administrative Tribunal for the judicial protection of officials'.[13]

69 The Court adopted the same approach in subsequent proceedings in 1973, receiving written submissions from both the Organization and the affected officials and rejecting a submission that it was required to afford an oral hearing.[14] In 1982, it adhered again to the same approach, finding that, in the exercise of its advisory opinion jurisdiction in such cases, 'actual equality should be ensured by practical measures'.[15] At the same time, it observed that such measures 'would need most careful reappraisal were the Court called upon to function as an appeal court in respect of the contentious case itself'.[16]

70 The Court revisited the whole question in 2012.[17] It concluded that 'questions may now properly be asked whether the system established in 1946 meets the present-day principle of

[10] *Judgments of the Administrative Tribunal of the ILO upon Complaints made against UNESCO* (Advisory Opinion) [1956] ICJ Rep 77 (noted Gross 1958). Article XII of the Statute of the ILOAT then provided that a participating international organisation that 'challenges a decision of the Tribunal confirming its jurisdiction, or considers that a decision of the Tribunal is vitiated by a fundamental fault in the procedure followed' might submit 'the question of the validity of the decision' to the ICJ for an advisory opinion. This provision was withdrawn by amendment on 7 June 2016.

[11] Ibid, 85.

[12] Ibid, 86.

[13] Idem.

[14] *Judgment No 158 of the United Nations Administrative Tribunal* (Advisory Opinion) [1973] ICJ Rep 166, [36].

[15] *Judgment No 273 of the United Nations Administrative Tribunal* (Advisory Opinion) [1982] ICJ Rep 325, [29] (noted Gomula 1991).

[16] Ibid, [59].

[17] *Judgment No 2867* (noted de Brabandere 2012; Vidal-Léon 2014).

equality of access to courts and tribunals. While the Court is not in a position to reform this system, it can attempt to ensure, so far as possible, that there is equality in the proceedings before it.'[18] Following this decision, the provisions in the Statutes of both the United Nations Administrative Tribunal (UNAT) and the ILOAT providing for a one-sided right of review by an international organization to the Court from judgments of the administrative tribunal have now been withdrawn. In the case of the UNAT, they have been replaced by a two-tier judicial system, with a right of appeal open to both parties.[19]

One of the arguments that the Court considered in its 2012 decision was a parallel alleged on behalf of the Organization, the International Fund for Agricultural Development ('the Fund') with investor–State arbitration. The Court distinguished the two processes in the following way: **71**

> In replying to the question about equality of access, the Fund emphasized what it saw as a parallel with investor–State arbitration. First, it pointed out that in such arbitrations, it is only the investor that may initiate the dispute settlement process. But that process is initiated in response to the conduct of the host State, alleged to be in breach of the investor's rights, and is a first instance process. It is comparable to the proceeding brought in the ILOAT by the staff member against the agency. In the case of investment arbitrations brought under the Convention on the Settlement of Investment Disputes between States and Nationals of Other States (United Nations Treaty Series (UNTS), Vol. 575, p. 159), both parties – and not just one – are able to seek interpretation, revision or annulment of the award: it is that situation which is analogous to the present one. The Fund, secondly, refers to a number of provisions in bilateral free trade and investment treaties which enable the State parties to those treaties, by joint decision, at the request of one of them, to declare their interpretation of a provision of the treaty. That interpretation is binding on the tribunal hearing an investment dispute including those brought by the investor. That situation bears little resemblance to the present one: parties to treaties are in general free to agree on their interpretation, while in the present case the Court is concerned with the initiation of a review process to be carried out by an independent tribunal.[20]

In these comments, the Court emphasises the central importance of the principle of equality to the design of the investment arbitration system under the ICSID Convention. **72**

What more conclusions of potential relevance to the present specific topic may be drawn from general international law? The principle of equality may be treated as a general principle of law governing the Court's procedures that is 'not solely a structural one, connected to the respective positions of the parties; it is also a substantive one, connected **73**

[18] Ibid, [44].

[19] Statute of the United Nations Appeals Tribunal adopted UNGA Res A/RES/63/253 (24 December 2008) as amended; Reinisch and Knahr 2008.

[20] *Judgment No 2867*, [43].

to the objectives of the procedure and the values of substantive justice'.[21] For this reason, it applies generally to all judicial or arbitral proceedings. But this does not imply inflexibility, since the principle must be applied in numerous practical contexts in which the court or tribunal is called upon to apply a fair procedure.

74 Equality in the Court's jurisprudence may be seen as having three dimensions: (1) as a constitutional principle; (2) as a principle of reciprocity; and (3) as a procedural principle:[22]

(1) *As a constitutional principle*, equality must be treated as superior to other procedural rules in light of its fundamental character. This was the conclusion that the Court adopted in its decisions on the anomalous use of its advisory opinion jurisdiction by international organizations to seek review of administrative tribunal judgments, reviewed above. The Court proactively limited the availability of oral argument and ensured that the officials had an equal opportunity to submit a written submission. In the end, its criticisms contributed to the withdrawal of the objectionable procedure.

(2) *As a principle of reciprocity*, equality operates generally to ensure that treatment accorded to one party (for example, in the granting of extensions of time or the admission of new evidence or submissions) is also accorded in substance to the other. In this regard, equality is closely linked to the principle of *audi alteram partem*: that the court or tribunal should always hear both sides, such that, if new evidence or explanations are admitted from one party, the other should equally have an opportunity to comment.[23] This principle is specifically enshrined in the Rules of the Court.[24] As Cheng observed, *audi alteram partem* 'may be regarded as a general principle of law translating into practice the fundamental requirement of equality between the parties in judicial proceedings'.[25]

(3) *As a procedural principle*, in ensuring substantial equality of treatment of the parties in the exercise of their procedural rights. As the Permanent Court observed, 'the Parties must have an equal opportunity reciprocally to discuss their respective contentions'.[26] The Court has frequently been called upon to apply considerations of equality to the procedures applied in specific cases. Its experience in this regard suggests that the principle cannot be applied rigidly. Flexibility must be preserved, having regard to the many different procedural postures that can arise in litigation before it. What is important is that substantial equality is maintained.

75 *International arbitration.* The principle of the equality of the parties is also fundamental to the conduct of international arbitration, as it has been developed for both inter-State disputes and international commercial disputes.

21 See Kolb 2013: 1119, for an illuminating analysis.

22 Ibid, 1123–7.

23 *Nuclear Tests (Australia v France, New Zealand v France)* [1974] ICJ Rep 253, [33]; *Legal Status of Eastern Greenland (Denmark v Norway)* (1933) PCIJ Rep, Ser A/B No 53, 25–6; *Chorzów Factory (Germany v Poland)* (Judgment on Merits) (1928) PCIJ Rep, Ser A No 17, 7, where the Permanent Court afforded a party a further opportunity to be heard on new evidence or submissions submitted by its opponent.

24 Arts 56(3) and 72, Rules of Court.

25 Cheng 1953: 291; accord: Mani 1980: 16.

26 *International Commission on the River Oder* (Order) (1929) PCIJ Rep, Ser A No 23, 45.

The Preamble to the International Law Commission's Model Rules on Arbitral Procedure states that: 'The undertaking to arbitrate is based on the following fundamental rules: . . . (5) The parties shall be equal in all proceedings before the arbitral tribunal.'[27] **76**

In explaining the basis for this rule, the Secretariat stated in its Commentary: **77**

> This article expresses a fundamental norm of procedure the observance of which is essential to the proper functioning of the tribunal. Implicit in the article is the principle that the treatment of the parties during the conduct of a case before the tribunal must be fully impartial. Yet something more than the notion of impartiality is involved; there is in addition the notion that there are certain basic principles of procedure which are indispensable conditions of the exercise by the tribunal of its jurisdiction. Thus a State is entitled to rely upon certain fundamental procedural rights in any international arbitration, of which no State would consent to be deprived. The procedural rights involved must, however, be fundamental in the sense that the interests of a party are materially affected, so as to go to the very root of the award.[28]

International arbitral practice in inter-State cases supports the proposition that an award may be invalid in cases of a serious departure from such a fundamental rule.[29] The ILC Model Rules provide that the validity of an award may be challenged if there has been 'a serious departure from a fundamental rule of procedure'.[30] The Secretariat Commentary identifies the '[r]ight of parties to equal and impartial treatment' and '[t]he right to be heard' as such fundamental rules of procedure.[31] **78**

In international commercial arbitration,[32] the equality principle is non-derogable. It qualifies the general rule that gives the tribunal broad power to conduct the arbitration as it considers appropriate. So, Article 17(1) (first sentence) of the UNCITRAL Rules 2010 (formerly Article 15(1) of the 1976 Rules) states: **79**

> Subject to these Rules, the arbitral tribunal may conduct the arbitration in such manner as it considers appropriate, *provided that the parties are treated with equality and that at an appropriate stage of the proceedings each party is given a reasonable opportunity of presenting its case.*[33]

27 International Law Commission, Model Rules on Arbitral Procedure [1958] 2 YB ILC 83.
28 ILC 1955: 55.
29 *La Constancia, Good Return and Medea (United States of America v Colombia)* (1866) 2 Moore 1396, XXIX RIAA 121; Carlston 1946: 39.
30 Art 35(c), ILC Model Rules.
31 ILC 1955: 110.
32 Bantekas 2020a.
33 Art 17(1), UNCITRAL Arbitration Rules as revised in 2010, adopted by UNGA Res 65/22 (6 December 2010) (emphasis added). The equivalent provision of the 1976 Rules, art 15(1), is to the same effect, save that 'at an appropriate stage' previously read 'at any stage'. See: Caron and Caplan 2013; Croft et al 2013: 173.

80 This provision is mirrored in Article 18 of the UNCITRAL Model Law, which provides that: 'The parties shall be treated with equality and each party shall be given a full opportunity of presenting his case.'[34]

81 The Tribunal in *Methanex v United States of America* underscored the importance of this rule holding:

> This provision [art 15(1) 1976 Rules] constitutes one of the essential 'hallmarks' of an international arbitration under the UNCITRAL Arbitration Rules, according to the *travaux préparatoires*. Article 15 has also been described as the 'heart' of the UNCITRAL Rules; and its terms have since been adopted in Articles 18 and 19(2) of the UNCITRAL Model Law on International Commercial Arbitration, where these provisions were considered as the procedural *'Magna Carta'* of international commercial arbitration.[35]

82 A fundamental breach of the equality principle constitutes the basis on which recognition and enforcement of an award may be refused on the ground provided in Article V(1)(b) of the New York Convention that: 'The party against whom the award is invoked was not given proper notice of the appointment of the arbitrator or of the arbitral proceedings or was otherwise unable to present his case.'[36] This provision permits a challenge to an award for 'a denial of procedural fairness, equality of treatment, or natural justice'.[37]

83 The equality principle in general international law is closely linked to other fundamental elements of a fair hearing, notably the requirement, enshrined in Article 14(1) ICCPR (second sentence) of 'a competent, independent and impartial tribunal'.

84 This principle, which is equally important, has been the subject of recent elaboration at the international level, including in a resolution of the *Institut*.[38] The two principles are especially closely linked through the element of judicial impartiality. This requires that the judge 'must not allow their judgement to be influenced by personal bias or prejudice, nor harbour preconceptions about the particular case before them, nor act in ways that improperly promote the interests of one party to the detriment of the other'.[39]

[34] Art 18, UNCITRAL Model Law on International Commercial Arbitration (adopted 21 June 1985, amended 7 July 2006) UN Docs A/40/17, annex I and A/61/17, annex I. See also Bantekas 2020: 522–38.

[35] *Methanex Corporation v United States of America* (Decision on *Amici Curiae*) (2001) 7 ICSID Rep 208 (NAFTA, Veeder P, Christopher & Rowley), [26].

[36] Art V(1)(b), Convention on the Recognition and Enforcement of Foreign Arbitral Awards (New York Convention) (signed 10 June 1958, entered into force 7 June 1959) 330 UNTS 38.

[37] Born 2014: 3494.

[38] Institut de Droit International 2011: 124; ILA 2005; IBA Guidelines 2014; and see art 8.30, CETA.

[39] UNHRC 2007: [21].

2 EQUALITY OF THE PARTIES AS A HUMAN RIGHT

Recital (2) refers to the principle of equality as it finds expression in the major international human rights instruments. Such provisions 'are relevant to the interpretation of the concept of a fundamental rule of procedure as used in Article 52(1)(d) of the ICSID Convention'.[40] **85**

Article 10 of the Universal Declaration of Human Rights provides: 'Everyone is entitled *in full equality* to a fair and public hearing by an independent and impartial tribunal, in the determination of his rights and obligations and of any criminal charge against him.'[41] Article 14(1) ICCPR opens: '*All persons shall be equal before the courts and tribunals.*'[42] **86**

The Human Rights Committee in its General Comment No 32 (adopted 23 August 2007) gives important guidance as to the proper interpretation of Article 14.[43] Although the focus of Article 14(1) and the General Comment is on the obligations of States to ensure equality before their national courts and tribunals, the Commentary provides useful insights as to the nature of the equality principle that may also assist in the interpretation of the principle of equality before international tribunals. **87**

The Committee observes that: 'The right to equality before the courts and tribunals and to a fair trial is a key element of human rights protection *and serves as a procedural means to safeguard the rule of law.*'[44] **88**

The Committee makes the following pertinent points specific to the first limb of the paragraph that protects the right to equality: **89**

(1) The right applies 'regardless of the nature of proceedings'.[45] It comprises equal access, equality of arms, treatment without discrimination and equality of proceedings.
(2) *Equal access* ensures that 'no individual is deprived, in procedural terms, of his/her right to claim justice'.[46] In the context of domestic proceedings, this means that a State may not discriminate as regards access to its courts and tribunals on grounds of nationality or otherwise. It 'prohibits any distinctions that are not based on law and cannot be justified on objective and reasonable grounds'.[47] While the obligations of States Parties vis-à-vis legal aid apply specifically only to criminal proceedings, equal access to other kinds of proceedings can be materially affected by such aid, since '[t]he availability or absence of legal assistance often determines whether or not a person can access the relevant proceedings or participate in them in a meaningful way'.[48]

40 *Tulip Real Estate Investment and Development Netherlands BV v Turkey* (Decision on Annulment) ICSID Case No ARB/11/28, IIC 756 (2015, Tomka P, Booth & Schreuer), [92].
41 Art 10, Universal Declaration of Human Rights 1948 UNGA Res 217A(III) (emphasis added).
42 Art 14(1), ICCPR (signed 16 December 1966, entered into force 23 March 1976) 999 UNTS 171 (emphasis added).
43 UNHRC 2007.
44 Ibid, [2] (emphasis added).
45 Ibid, [3].
46 Ibid, [9].
47 Idem.
48 Ibid, [10].

(3) Equality of arms 'means that the same procedural rights are to be provided to all the parties unless distinctions are based on law and can be justified on objective and reasonable grounds, not entailing actual disadvantage'.[49] In civil proceedings, equality of arms 'demands, inter alia, that each side be given the opportunity to contest all the arguments and evidence adduced by the other party'.[50]

(4) *Equality of proceedings.* Finally, '[e]quality before courts and tribunals also requires that similar cases are dealt with in similar proceedings'.[51]

90 That equal treatment 'includes avoidance of any kind of illegitimate discrimination, particularly on the basis of nationality or residence' is supported by the ALI/UNIDROIT Principles of Transnational Civil Procedure.[52]

91 The fundamental character of the principle of 'equality of arms' is such that, even where it is not expressly mentioned, it has been found to be an inherent component of the right to a fair hearing. So, for example, Article 6 of the European Convention on Human Rights, which guarantees a fair hearing, does not explicitly mention the equality of the parties.[53] Nevertheless, the European Commission on Human Rights held at any early stage that the principle is part of the right to a fair hearing,[54] a finding that was endorsed by the Court.[55]

49 Ibid, [13].

50 Idem.

51 Ibid, [14].

52 Principle 3.2, ALI/UNIDROIT 2004: 20–1.

53 Art 6, Convention for the Protection of Human Rights and Fundamental Freedoms (ECHR) (signed 4 November 1950, entered into force 3 September 1953) 213 UNTS 221.

54 *X v Austria* App No 1747/62 (ECommHR, 1963); *Neumeister v Austria* App No 1936/63 (ECommHR, 1964) 7 YB 224.

55 *Neumeister v Austria* (ECtHR, 1968) ECHR Ser A No 8, 39, [22]; Schabas 2015: 288.

B Part One: Application to the Establishment of the Tribunal

CHAPTER I: FORUM

ARTICLE I:

Legal Character

(1) The extent to which a dispute between the national of one State ('the investor') and another State ('the State') in respect of an investment may be submitted to the jurisdiction of an international investment tribunal ('the tribunal') results from the scope of the parties' consent. Submission of such a dispute to the tribunal engages the principle of the equality of the parties.

(2) Such a forum is designed to secure equality between the parties in circumstances where the State has the sovereign power to enforce its own law and adjudicate its claims against investors for breach of its laws before its own courts.

The operative text of the resolution is divided into two parts: **92**

(1) Part One concerns the establishment of the tribunal. It addresses the constitutional aspects of the equality principle. It is divided into two chapters: (1) on forum; (2) on the tribunal, each of which contains two articles.

(2) Part Two concerns the application of equality to the procedure of the tribunal. It contains three chapters: (1) on the parties; (2) on pleading and evidence; and (3) on substantive equality of arms.

Chapter One of Part One addresses two fundamental threshold issues as to the predicates for **93** the engagement of the equality principle (Article 1) and its implications for access (Article 2).

Paragraph (1) of Article 1 does not prescribe the manner in which the parties' consent to **94** submit an investment dispute to an international tribunal may be given or defined. Its purpose is rather to confirm that the jurisdiction of an international investment tribunal is always dependent upon the scope of the parties' consent. Once so submitted, the principle of the equality of the parties is engaged.

Paragraph (2) contains two interlinked elements: **95**

(1) In the first place, it confirms that the international investment tribunal provides a forum for the resolution of investment disputes that, in common with other international courts and tribunals, ensures the equality of the parties.

(2) In the second place, as the jurisdiction of such a tribunal depends upon the consent of the State, it respects the fact that the State retains the power to enforce its own law and adjudicate its claims against investors for breach of its laws before its own courts.

96 This second clause of paragraph (2) is one of several places in the resolution which serve to underscore the point that, while procedural equality is an essential attribute of a fair system of adjudication which must be applied to investment tribunals, this does not change the fact that, as observed in recital (7) of the preamble, the two parties have a different juridical character. While the State may validly choose to consent to submit a dispute with an investor to the jurisdiction of an investment tribunal, it retains the sovereign power, should it prefer to do so, to bring its own claim against an investor before its own national courts according to national law. This point is pursued further in Article 2(1) and (2).

ARTICLE 2:
Access

(1) **Both the State and the investor are equally entitled to submit a claim in relation to an investment to a tribunal, subject to the terms of the instrument of consent, interpreted in accordance with the principle of the equality of the parties.**

(2) **No State is obliged to submit its claim against an investor to a tribunal, unless it gives its consent and elects to do so. Otherwise, a State remains entitled to use the rights and remedies provided by its own national legal system in order to pursue such a claim before its own courts.**

(3) **The limitation of access to the investor of another State bears a direct relationship to the object of investment treaties, which is to promote and protect foreign investment and the rights of foreign nationals, while also respecting the State's sovereign right to regulate investment activities within its jurisdiction in the public interest. It does not infringe the principle of equality of access. Such protection is equally available to the investors of each State when they make an investment within the scope of the treaty protections by investing in the territory of the other State.**

Equality of access to investment arbitration falls to be considered at two levels: (1) **97** as between the investor and the State in the institution of a claim; and (2) as between investors of different nationality – domestic and foreign. Article 2 considers each of these aspects. Paragraphs (1) and (2) of Article 2 concern equality of access as between investor and State. Paragraph (3) deals with the requirement of foreign nationality.

1 The Institution of a Claim

Paragraph (1) states the basic principle that equality of access applies to the **98** submission of an investment claim. This is subject to the proviso that the tribunal's jurisdiction depends upon the scope of consent, which may itself limit which claims may be brought.

The equality principle is applied in the ICSID Convention. A request for arbitration under the **99** Convention may be addressed to the Secretary-General *either* by a Contracting State *or* by a national of a Contracting State.[56] In other words, the Convention may be asymmetric, but it is not – at least in its design – one-sided. Broches emphasised that the wide enforceability of awards in the territories of other Contracting States 'was inserted primarily with the needs of host States in mind'.[57] In practice, however, this ambition of the framers has not been

[56] Art 36(1), ICSID Convention.
[57] Art 54; Broches 1972: 349.

realised. States have made almost no use of the Convention as original claimants against investors.[58]

100 *Paragraph (2)*: The availability of international investment arbitration to address the claims of both investors and host States is limited by the decisions of States as to the circumstances in which they are prepared to confer jurisdiction upon the tribunal. The ICSID Convention expressly confirms that 'no Contracting State shall by the mere fact of its ratification, acceptance or approval of this Convention and without its consent be deemed to be under any obligation to submit any particular dispute to conciliation or arbitration'.[59]

101 The consequence is that the State's consent must always be given in writing in a separate instrument, which will determine the scope of the disputes submitted to arbitration.[60] The dispute settlement clause is separable from the substantive provisions of the investment agreement – contract or treaty – in which it is contained.[61]

102 Arbitration is a remedy that is alternative to other forms of relief. In many instances in which States themselves have a claim against an investor, they may choose to pursue that claim before their national courts. The ICSID Convention does not generally preclude that course.[62] The jurisdiction of the Centre exists only in respect of a dispute 'which the parties to the dispute consent in writing to submit to the Centre'.[63] As a result, resort to arbitration under the Convention requires both the consent of the State and the consent of the investor.

103 Where the State's consent is given in a contract between it and the foreign investor, the synallagmatic character of the rights and duties contained in the contract will of their nature be equally open to vindication at the suit of the investor or the State according to the law applicable to that contract.[64]

104 Where, however, the State's consent is given in an investment treaty:

[58] Schreuer et al 2009: 458. An attempt on the part of a provincial government to invoke ICSID jurisdiction against the investor on a contract claim failed on grounds of lack of consent and standing to represent the State under art 25 of the ICSID Convention: *Government of the Province of East Kalimantan v PT Kaltim Prima Coal* (Award on Jurisdiction) ICSID Case No ARB/07/3 (2009, Kaufmann-Kohler P, Hwang & van den Berg). The scope of host States' ability to pursue counterclaims will be considered below in the commentary on Art 6.

[59] Preamble, Recital 7, ICSID Convention.

[60] Art 25(1), ICSID Convention.

[61] *Elf Aquitaine Iran v National Iranian Oil Co* (Preliminary Award) XI YB Comm Arb 97 (14 January 1982), [256]; Schreuer et al 2009: 260, [25.622]; *Duke Energy International Peru Investments No 1 Ltd v Peru* (Decision on Annulment) ICSID Case No ARB/03/28 (2011, McLachlan P, Hascher & Tomka), [131].

[62] Save to the extent that it conflicts with the concurrent pursuit by the investor of a parallel claim before ICSID once instituted, in light of the assurance of exclusivity of remedy that States give when they consent to arbitration pursuant to Article 26: Schreuer et al 2009: 351.

[63] Art 25(1), ICSID Convention.

[64] Art 42, ICSID Convention.

(1) The arbitration agreement in the treaty may provide that any dispute between an investor and the State concerning the investment may be submitted by either party to arbitration.[65] In this event, the scope of the submission to arbitration is fully bilateral and the source of the legal obligations to be invoked is not prescribed by the terms of the consent, but rather is limited by the subject matter, namely, the investment.

(2) In a second scenario, which typifies the current structure of many investment treaties,[66] States have chosen to give their consent to the arbitration of disputes solely at the suit of the investor and normally only for the vindication of the rights protected by the treaty.

It is this second category of investment treaties that has given rise to the majority of investment claims. The legal character of such claims is of its nature unilateral, since the purpose of the protections contained in such treaties is to maintain a certain level of 'external control over the host States' actions in light of certain obligations that it cannot change unilaterally. Such obligations and external control are consented by the host State in order to attract foreign investment and depoliticize potential disputes that could otherwise be channelled through diplomatic protection claims initiated by the investor's State.'[67] **105**

The legal character of this type of claim does not engage or imperil the equality of the parties. It is the result of the deliberate choices that States have made in the design of the remedy that they have agreed to provide. In this respect, international investment arbitration is similar to international human rights adjudication, which is alike concerned with securing some external control over the actions of States in respect of obligations from which they may not derogate at international law. Indeed, this form of investment treaty is designed to secure a measure of equality between the parties in circumstances where the State otherwise has the sovereign power to enforce its own law and adjudicate its claims against investors for breach of its laws before its own courts. **106**

Such a limitation of claims and of access is a matter of the choices made by States in treaty design. States may, if they so choose, agree to impose obligations upon each other's investors as a condition of investment. Increasing attention is being given to this possibility in the literature.[68] To date, however, there have been only limited attempts to define the substantive content and procedural consequences of such an approach in the treaty practice of States.[69] **107**

65 See, e.g., Art 8, France Model BIT; McLachlan et al 2017: App 10; Art X(1), US–Argentina BIT (signed 14 November 1991, entered into force 20 October 1994) Senate Treaty Doc 103–02, considered in *Urbaser SA v Argentina* (Award) ICSID Case No ARB/07/26 (2016, Bucher P, Martinez-Fraga & McLachlan), [1143].

66 See, e.g., Art 26(2), Energy Charter Treaty (ECT) (signed 17 December 1994, entered into force 16 April 1998) 2080 UNTS 100; art 32, ASEAN Comprehensive Investment Agreement (signed 26 February 2009, entered into force 29 March 2012); art 24, US Revised Model BIT 2012, McLachlan et al 2017: App 6; art 10, Germany Model BIT, ibid: App 7. Some other BITs provide an equal right to investors and States to submit claims: art 8, UK Model BIT 2008, ibid: App 4; art 8, France Model BIT, ibid: App 10.

67 d'Argent (2019) 79 *Annuaire* 545; and see, to like effect, Stern 2009: 96–7.

68 Amado et al 2018; Boisson de Chazournes 2018.

69 See notably the Draft Pan-African Investment Code (adopted 21–23 November 2016, not yet in force) Ch 4; on which, see: Shaw Kern 2019; Mbengue and Schacherer 2018: 547.

108 At the same time, in drafting the treaty, States themselves may also decide whether in principle this is a forum to which they themselves wish to be able to resort.

109 The current forms of dispute settlement clauses in those treaties or drafts that contemplate the establishment of a standing investment tribunal are one-way clauses. The Canada–EU Comprehensive Economic and Trade Agreement (CETA) limits access to its dispute resolution procedures to cases in which 'an investor of the Party' submits 'a claim that the other Party has breached an obligation' under the Treaty 'where the investor claims to have suffered loss or damage as a result of the alleged breach'.[70]

110 A general bilateral disputes clause provides equally for resort to dispute resolution by either the State or the investor. The consent of the investor is also necessary to complete the arbitration agreement. But the consent of the State is not limited either to disputes in respect of obligations under the treaty or to disputes instituted by investors. The one-way clause is, by contrast, limited in both of these respects. As will be seen below, this choice of consent clause affects the extent to which the State may pursue a counterclaim.

111 State-owned enterprises have sued as claimants. But they have done so in their capacity as commercial investors against host States. Tribunals have generally accepted this, provided that the claimant is bringing suit in respect of activities that are essentially commercial rather than governmental in nature.[71] The extent to which the admission of such claims is permissible (in view of the fact that the Convention is concerned solely with 'private international investment'[72] and implicitly excludes inter-State claims) is a matter of some controversy.[73]

112 The decision of States not to resort to investment arbitration as claimants, save where they are themselves investors, is because States have generally preferred to use the rights and remedies provided by their own national legal systems in order to pursue claims against investors and to do so in their own courts. Save in the case of contractual disputes (where submission to international arbitration continues to be common[74]) and counterclaims (considered further under Article 6), a decision to refer such disputes to international arbitration rather than the national courts of the host State might itself raise significant sovereignty implications. It might suggest that the State itself had a lack of confidence in its own courts and might also be seen as enabling foreign investors to escape responsibility for their own actions before local courts. In principle, States have a responsibility to use their

[70] Art 8.18, CETA.

[71] *Ceskoslovenska Obchodni Banka AS v Slovakia* (Decision on Jurisdiction) ICSID Case No ARB/97/4, 5 ICSID Rep 330 (1999, Buergenthal P, Bernardini & Bucher), [17]; *Beijing Urban Construction Group Co Ltd v Yemen* (Decision on Jurisdiction) ICSID Case No ARB/14/30, IIC 949 (2017, Binnie P, Douglas & Townsend), [31], [39]; Schreuer et al 2009: 161–2.

[72] Preamble Recital 1, ICSID Convention.

[73] Chaise and Sejko 2016; Feldman 2016; Poulsen 2016.

[74] Brower and Kumar 2015; ICC 2012.

domestic legal system to ensure accountability of private persons, including business enterprises.[75]

Nevertheless, there remain sound practical reasons why a State might wish to consider submitting its claim against an investor to international arbitration. The foreign investor (as distinct from its local investment vehicle) may well have no presence within the jurisdiction of the host State. The States Parties to the ICSID Convention have assumed an obligation to 'recognize an award as binding and enforce the pecuniary obligations imposed by that award within its territories as if it were a final judgment of a court of that State'.[76] The international enforceability of an ICSID arbitral award far exceeds the enforceability of the judgment of any national court. **113**

2 *The Condition of Foreign Nationality*

Paragraph (3) addresses the important threshold question of whether the limitation of access to investors of another State, which is an integral feature of international investment protection, is consistent with the equality principle. **114**

The ICSID Convention was deliberately designed to limit the availability of its procedures to a particular class of individuals, namely 'national[s] of another Contracting State'.[77] This is inherent in the whole structure of the Convention, finding expression in its title and in its operative jurisdictional provisions. It reflects the Convention's origins as a new form of dispute resolution to address an existing category of obligations of States under international law in the treatment of aliens and their property.[78] **115**

Access is not open to nationals of the host State. In the framing of the Convention, 'there was a widespread recognition that it was unrealistic to expect a State to submit to an international jurisdiction with respect to its own national'.[79] As a result, Article 25(2)(a) specifically states that the national of another Contracting State 'does not include any person who . . . also had the nationality of the Contracting State party to the dispute'. **116**

The Report of the Executive Directors is categorical about this limitation: **117**

> [A] natural person who was a national of the State party to the dispute would not be eligible to be a party in proceedings under the auspices of the Centre,

75 See, e.g., Principle 1, United Nations, 'Guiding Principles on Business and Human Rights' (the Ruggie Commission) (2011) UN Doc HR/PUB/11/04 ('States must protect against human rights abuse within their territory and/or jurisdiction by third parties, including business enterprises. This requires taking appropriate steps to prevent, investigate, punish and redress such abuse through effective policies, legislation, regulations and adjudication.').

76 Art 43(1), ICSID Convention.

77 Art 25, ICSID Convention.

78 Jennings and Watts 1992: vol 1, 924–5.

79 Schreuer et al 2009: 271.

> even if at the same time he had the nationality of another State. This ineligibility is absolute and cannot be cured even if the State party to the dispute had given its consent.[80]

118 Article 25(2)(b) contains a limited extension in the case of juridical persons that are nationals of the home State. This does not affect the underlying principle. The extension only applies to such person that 'because of foreign control, the parties have agreed should be treated as a national of another Contracting State for the purpose of the Convention'.[81]

119 At this constitutional level, investment arbitration operates on a quite different basis from international human right protections that apply regardless of nationality. So, for example, Article 2(1) of the ICCPR (adopted in 1966, the year following the conclusion of the ICSID Convention) provides:

> Each State Party to the present Covenant undertakes to respect and to ensure to all individuals within its territory and subject to its jurisdiction the rights recognised in the present Covenant, without distinction of any kind, such as race, colour, sex, language, religion, political or other opinion, national or social origin, property, birth or other state.

120 Where an international human rights tribunal has been endowed with jurisdiction to determine individual complaints, it will be competent to hear cases brought by a national of the respondent State. Such cases may include claims by host State nationals for breaches of the right to a fair hearing and for the protection of private property that are in substance closely related to the rights enshrined in investment treaties for the protection of foreign nationals only.[82]

121 The Human Rights Committee regards equal access to a tribunal without discrimination and equality of proceedings as elements of the right to a fair trial.[83]

122 The limitations on access to foreign nationals contained in the ICSID Convention may be explained by the Convention's origins as an attempt to address specific problems that had otherwise been encountered in the protection of foreign private investment and the resolution of disputes on a level playing field between foreign investors and States arising from such investment.[84] In other words, it was seen as an attempt to apply the equality principle as between the State and the foreign investor to this class of disputes.

80 ICSID 1965: [29].

81 For discussion, see McLachlan et al 2017: [5.134]–[5.153].

82 Art 6 and First Protocol, Art 1, ECHR; see, e.g., *Yukos Oil OAO v Russia* ECtHR App No 14902/04 (Admissibility) 29 January 2009, (Merits) 20 September 2011, [516]–[526], (Just satisfaction) 24 June 2014.

83 UNHRC 2007, General Comment No 32, [9], [14].

84 Broches 1972: 343–4.

The Convention does so by creating a specific forum that is available only with the consent of the State as an alternative to other fora for the resolution of a dispute between a foreign investor and the State.[85] ICSID arbitration operates, where such consent is given, in substitution for, and to the exclusion of, national remedies in the host State.[86] Unless the host State has expressly so stated as a condition of its consent, there is no requirement to exhaust local remedies.[87] It also excludes the exercise of the home State's right to espouse an international claim by way of diplomatic protection, a right that is of its nature limited by the bond of nationality.[88] **123**

One of the grounds of academic and public opposition to investment arbitration has been its differential access for foreign investors. For example, the Toronto Declaration states: 'All investors, regardless of nationality, should have access to an open and independent judicial system for the resolution of disputes, including disputes with government.'[89] The Declaration adds that private individuals, local communities and civil society organisations should have a 'full and equal participation ... alongside the investor where their interests are affected'. **124**

Although this argument takes a number of different forms, it is more usually expressed as an objection *in limine* to the ability of foreign investors to circumvent national courts through resort to international arbitration.[90] **125**

The reform proposals currently being advanced at the international level do not at present address this objection.[91] They do not propose to extend access to an international investment tribunal beyond the category of disputes between States and nationals of other States.[92] Nor do they propose to endow national courts with competence to enforce rights under investment treaties.[93] Nor do they propose to replace this system with one of inter-State claims, whether by way of diplomatic protection or the vindication of the direct rights of States.[94] Rather, they presume a continued role for an international tribunal to resolve specifically international disputes on the international plane between, on the one hand, a State and, on the other, the nationals of another State. **126**

85 Art 25(1).
86 Art 26.
87 Idem.
88 Art 27(1).
89 'An Open Letter about Investor–State Dispute Settlement' (20 April 2015), www.osgoode.yorku.ca/public-statement-international-investment-regime-31-august-2010. The Declaration nevertheless continues to accept a role for contract-based arbitration of investment contracts.
90 EC 2015: 34, 133.
91 Roberts 2018: 417.
92 Geneva CIDS (Kaufmann-Kohler and Potestà) 2016; UNCITRAL Report 2017a.
93 Current EU treaty practice limits such competence at present: Bronckers 2015; Semertzi 2014.
94 Cf. the (currently limited) position of investment within the WTO system: Agreement on Trade-Related Investment Measures (TRIMS) (signed 15 April 1994), Annex 1A to Marrakesh Agreement establishing the World Trade Organization 1868 UNTS 186. But see now WTO 2017: [1.4]–[1.6], which states that 'trade and investment are inseparable', 'highlighted the importance of advancing regional and international co-operation to create a more transparent, efficient, and predictable environment for investment and trade' and 'urged WTO Members to undertake more focused discussions aimed at developing a multilateral framework to facilitate investment for development'.

127 This fundamental aspect of the constitutional design of an investment court has not gone unchallenged. It has been the subject of constitutional challenges to the ratification of CETA within the European Union and its Member States. The provisions of Chapter 8, which establish the Investment Court, will not be provisionally applied and will not enter into force until ratified by all Member States.[95]

128 In *France*, the *Conseil Constitutionnel* addressed whether the inclusion in CETA of provision for an international investment tribunal open only to foreign investors and not to domestic investors was contrary to Article 6 of the Declaration of 1789, which requires that the law '*doit être la même pour tous, soit qu'elle protège, soit qu'elle punisse*'.[96]

129 The Council held that the equality principle is not infringed by such a system. In an important passage, it held that the Treaty has as its substantive object an assurance of the provision of the same treatment for foreign investors as for nationals. The limitation of the international forum to foreign investors has a direct connection with the object of the treaty to promote investment exchanges between the parties and operates on the basis of reciprocity, being equally open to French nationals investing in Canada:[97]

> 35. . . . Le principe d'égalité ne s'oppose ni à ce que le législateur règle de façon différente des situations différentes ni à ce qu'il déroge à l'égalité pour des raisons d'intérêt général, pourvu que, dans l'un et l'autre cas, la différence de traitement qui en résulte soit en rapport direct avec l'objet de la loi qui l'établit.
>
> 36. En premier lieu, les stipulations du chapitre 8 de l'accord comportent, en faveur des investisseurs non ressortissants de l'État d'accueil de l'investissement, des prescriptions touchant à certains droits substantiels. Celles-ci, qui sont relatives en particulier au traitement national, au traitement de la nation la plus favorisée, au traitement juste et équitable et à la protection contre les expropriations directes ou indirectes, ont pour seul objet d'assurer à ces investisseurs des droits dont bénéficient les investisseurs nationaux. Ainsi, le a du paragraphe 6 de l'instrument interprétatif commun prévoit que l'accord « *ne conduira pas à accorder un traitement plus favorable aux investisseurs étrangers qu'aux investisseurs nationaux* ». Dès lors, les stipulations du chapitre 8 ne créent sur ce point aucune différence de traitement.
>
> 37. En second lieu, en revanche, la section F du chapitre 8 crée une différence de traitement entre les personnes investissant en France en réservant l'accès aux tribunaux qu'elle institue aux seuls investisseurs canadiens.
>
> 38. Cette différence de traitement entre les investisseurs canadiens et les autres investisseurs étrangers en France répond toutefois au double motif d'intérêt général tenant, d'un côté, à créer, de manière réciproque, un cadre protecteur pour les investisseurs français au Canada et, de l'autre, à attirer les investissements canadiens en France.

95 Art 1(1)(a), Council Decision (EU) 2017/38 (28 October 2016) OJ L 11/1080 (14 January 2017). See also Riffel 2020.

96 CC 31 July 2017 No 2017–749 DC.

97 Ibid, [35]–[40].

> 39. Ce motif d'intérêt général étant en rapport direct avec l'objet de l'accord, qui est de favoriser les échanges entre les parties, les stipulations du chapitre 8 pouvaient donc instituer un mécanisme procédural de règlement des différends susceptible de s'appliquer, s'agissant d'investissements réalisés en France, aux seuls investisseurs canadiens.
>
> 40. Il résulte de ce qui précède que les stipulations du chapitre 8 de l'accord ne méconnaissent pas le principe d'égalité devant la loi.

In *Germany*, the *Bundesverfassungsgericht* considered a similar question in the context of a reference on the compatibility of the investor–State provisions in CETA with the German Constitution.[98] **130**

In *Belgium*, the Federal Government requested an Opinion from the Court of Justice of the European Union (CJEU) on the compatibility of the proposed Investment Court System with the European Treaties.[99] One of the issues on which the Court's Opinion was sought was whether such a system is compatible with the general principle of equality.[100] **131**

On 29 January 2019, Advocate General Bot delivered an Opinion concluding that the provisions of Chapter 8 of CETA did not infringe the general principle of equal treatment.[101] The Opinion held that: **132**

> 205. It would, in any event, be wrong to take the view that, given their ability to bring matters before the CETA Tribunal, Canadian undertakings investing in the European Union are placed in a preferential situation as compared with EU undertakings investing in the European Union. That possibility merely compensates for the fact that the CETA cannot be relied on directly before the domestic courts and tribunals of the Parties.
>
> . . .

98 *CETA (re: Approval of Germany)* 2 BvR 1368/16, 2 BvR 1444/16, 2 BvR 1482/16, 2 BvE 3/16 (7 December 2016) ECLI:DE:BVerfG:2016:rs20161207.2bvr144416, rejecting the applications for a preliminary injunction to restrain the Federal Government from voting in favour of the adoption of CETA in the European Council. The Court earlier rejected an application for a preliminary injunction in relation to the same question on 13 October 2016: ECLI:DE:BVerfG:2016:rs20161013.2bvr136816.

99 *Opinion 1/17* OJ 2017/C/369/2.

100 'CETA: Belgian Request for an Opinion from the European Court of Justice' (6 September 2017), 2, https://diplomatie.belgium.be/sites/default/files/downloads/ceta_summary.pdf. In Case C-284/16 *Slovak Republic v Achmea*, the European Court was asked whether the investor–State mechanism in an intra-EU BIT was contrary to EU law, inter alia, because it afforded a right to the nationals of one member State that was not available to the nationals of other Member States. Wathelet A-G expressed the Opinion (19 September 2017, EU:C:2017: 699) that 'there is no discrimination prohibited by EU law' inherent in such a provision: [65]. It was inherent in the bilateral nature of the BIT and such distinctions had been accepted by the Court in the context of double-tax treaties. The CJEU did not then express a view on this question, as it found the intra-EU BIT to be incompatible with EU law on other grounds: (6 March 2018, EU:C:2018:158) [2018] 4 WLR 87. In *Opinion 1/17*, the CJEU distinguished the investment court system in CETA from the investment agreement at issue in *Achmea*, as the former concerns an agreement between the European Union and a non-Member State, rather than an agreement between EU Member States: [126]–[127].

101 *Opinion 1/17* (29 January 2019, ECLI:EU:C:2019:72, Opinion Bot A-G), [213].

> 207. . . . the situation of Canadian investors who invest in the European Union is not comparable with the situation of European investors who invest within their own economic area. Canadian or European investors can be compared only in relation to the investments which they make in the territory of the other Party. On the basis of that comparison, all investors who are in a comparable situation are treated comparably . . .

133 On 30 April 2019, the CJEU rendered *Opinion 1/17*, in which the Full Court held that CETA's Investment Court System was compatible with the principle of equal treatment.[102] The Court adopted a similar analysis to that of Bot A-G cited above. It added that the difference in treatment 'is, in any event, justified by the objective of contributing to free and fair trade'. It pointed out that the competence of the Union to conclude agreements concerning direct investments with non-Member States 'would be meaningless if the EU law principle of equal treatment were to prohibit the Union from entering into specific commitments with respect to investments deriving from non-Member States'.[103]

134 In conclusion, the limitation of access to foreign investors that is a cardinal feature of international investment arbitration does not implicate or infringe the equality principle. It bears a direct relationship to the object of investment treaties, which is to promote and protect *foreign* investment. Such protection is equally available to the investors of each State when they make an investment within the scope of the treaty protections: by investing in the territory of the other State.

135 States have constantly insisted on the nationality requirement in investment arbitration in order to resist the possibility of claims by domestic investors.[104] They have also crafted treaty provisions, notably denial of benefits clauses that are designed to protect against abuses of the nationality requirement by corporate claimants.[105] Much of that drafting work has been concerned with ensuring that the nationality requirement is strictly policed in substance and not only in form, rather than with its relaxation.

136 It would in theory be possible to extend the investment arbitration mechanism to domestic as well as international investors, in the same way as has been the case with international human rights complaints mechanisms. But this would have very wide policy implications for the integrity of States' domestic legal systems: much wider implications than the existing system of limited protections for foreign investment. Such a protection is directly connected to a basic function of international law – namely, the protection of aliens against the abuse of power by States other than their home State.

137 The availability of a direct right of action on the part of investors is a procedural means of securing that purpose.

102 *Opinion 1/17* (CJEU) (30 April 2019, ECLI:EU:C:2019:341), [2020] 59 ILM 89, [79]–[84].
103 Ibid, [84].
104 For a full analysis of the authorities, see McLachlan et al 2017: ch 5.
105 See, e.g., Art 17(2), US Model BIT 2012; McLachlan et al 2017: App 6; art 9.15(2), Comprehensive and Progressive Trans-Pacific Partnership Agreement (signed 8 March 2018, entered into force 30 December 2018) (CPTPP).

CHAPTER 2: TRIBUNAL

ARTICLE 3

Impartiality

(1) **The impartiality of all members of a tribunal is an indispensable prerequisite to the equality of the parties.**
(2) **The substantive standards applicable to the determination of any question relating to the impartiality of a member of an arbitral tribunal should be uniform and transparent.**
(3) **The IBA Guidelines on Conflicts of Interest in International Arbitration 2014 provide a useful framework of substantive rules within which to analyse questions that may arise as to the impartiality of a member of an arbitral tribunal constituted to decide an investment dispute.**
(4) **Challenges to the impartiality of a member of an arbitral tribunal should be determined by an independent third party decision-maker external to the tribunal.**
(5) **As a consequence States parties to the ICSID Convention are encouraged to amend Article 58 so as to refer the determination of challenge applications to an independent third party decision-maker in all cases.**

The appointment to and design of an international investment tribunal raises important questions of the constitutional application of the equality principle. Here, equality can connote two different ideas: **138**

(1) *Equality of treatment* – that the members appointed to a tribunal must be impartial, treating each party equally in their consideration of the claims placed before them for adjudication; and
(2) *Equality of appointment* – that the parties should have an equal right to participate in the appointment of tribunal members.

Equality of treatment and impartiality are dealt with in Article 3. The application of the equality principle in the context of the appointment of the tribunal (though it logically arises first) is dealt with in Article 4, as it gives rise to larger issues concerning the composition of any permanent tribunal as compared with arbitral tribunals. **139**

Article 3 is divided into five paragraphs. It is concerned with three topics: **140**

(1) The relation of the impartiality of the tribunal to the principle of equality – paragraph (1);
(2) The substantive standards applicable to the determination of impartiality – paragraphs (2) and (3);
(3) The method for the determination of challenges to impartiality – (4) and (5).

1 The Standard of Impartiality

141 Equality of treatment is an indispensable requirement of any fair system of adjudication, whether by arbitral tribunals or standing courts and tribunals. Article 10 of the Universal Declaration links equality and impartiality in prescribing that: 'Everyone is entitled in full equality to a fair and public hearing by an independent and impartial tribunal, in the determination of his rights and obligations.'[106] While arbitration is not required to be public, the independence and impartiality of an arbitrator is considered to be a fundamental rule of procedure, without which there can be no right to a fair trial or a right of fair defence. It 'goes to the very heart of the integrity of arbitral procedure'.[107]

142 Independence and impartiality are distinct but related concepts. As it was put in *Suez v Argentina*:

> The concepts of independence and impartiality, though related, are often seen as distinct, although the precise nature of the distinction is not always easy to grasp. Generally speaking, independence relates to the lack of relations with a party that might influence an arbitrator's decision. Impartiality, on the other hand, concerns the absence of a bias or predisposition toward one of the parties.[108]

143 While there is undoubtedly a close relation between the two concepts, Article 3 focuses on impartiality, since it is this criterion that is most connected to the equality of the parties.

144 The issues that have arisen under this head in investment arbitration have focused on: (1) the definition of what conduct is capable of giving rise to a conflict of interest that might justifiably cause the impartiality of an arbitrator to be called into question; and (2) the most appropriate process by which challenges to impartiality are to be determined.

145 The most commonly applied reference point for the substantive content of conduct giving rise to a conflict of interest is the IBA Guidelines on Conflicts of Interest in International Arbitration. These were revised in 2014. They expressly confirm that they 'apply to international commercial arbitration *and investment arbitration*'.[109]

146 In the context of ICSID proceedings, Arbitration Rule 6 requires each arbitrator to sign a declaration confirming, inter alia, that he or she 'shall judge fairly as between the parties',

106 Art 10, UDHR.

107 *EDF International SA v Argentina* (Annulment Decision) ICSID Case No ARB/03/23 (2013, Greenwood P, Cheng & Taniguchi), [123]; see also: UNCITRAL 2019b, UN Doc A/CN.9/WG.III/WP.167, [15]–[19]; *Eiser Infrastructure Ltd v Spain* (Decision on Annulment) ICSID Case No ARB/13/36 (2020, Ramírez Hernández, P, Ali Khan & Hascher).

108 *Suez v Argentina* (Disqualification Proposal Decision) ICSID Case No ARB/03/17 (2007, Salacuse P & Nikken) [29].

109 IBA Guidelines 2014: Introduction, [5] (emphasis added). Art 8.30(1), CETA incorporates these Guidelines until the Committee on Services and Investment adopts a code of conduct for Tribunal Members under art 8.44(2).

disclosing 'any other circumstance that may cause [his or her] reliability for independent judgment to be questioned by a party'. Article 57 of the ICSID Convention provides that the appointment of an arbitrator may be challenged for 'manifest lack of the qualities required by paragraph (1) of Article 14', which include that the person 'may be relied upon to exercise independent judgment'.

The ICSID Secretariat Note on the current text of Arbitration Rule 6 conforms the test for disclosure in ICSID proceedings to that applicable under the UNCITRAL Rules and in the IBA Guidelines on Conflicts of Interest in International Arbitration 2014, namely that the facts are 'likely to give rise to justifiable doubts' as to the arbitrator's impartiality or independence.[110] **147**

The review standard provided under Article 57 of the ICSID Convention in the event of a challenge to an arbitrator requires that the arbitrator's lack of the requisite qualities must be 'manifest'. The question whether this mandates a higher test to the 'justifiable doubts' test applicable in arbitration generally (including in investment arbitration outside the ICSID Convention) has been a matter of some doubt in the jurisprudence.[111] **148**

It is submitted that this qualification is designed to ensure that the *evidence* for lack of impartiality must be clear; it does not suggest that lack of impartiality can be a matter of degree.[112] In principle, a single coherent standard is essential to the sound administration of justice. **149**

At the same time, the fact that a matter is disclosed or not disclosed cannot be determinative of whether a lack of impartiality is, in fact established, since, as the comments to the IBA Guidelines themselves state, 'disclosure does not imply the existence of a conflict of interest' and, furthermore, 'a failure to disclose certain facts and circumstances that may, in the eyes of the parties, give rise to doubts as to the arbitrator's impartiality or independence, does not necessarily mean that a conflict of interest exists, or that a disqualification should ensue'.[113] **150**

110 ICSID Working Paper, 'Suggested Changes to the ICSID Rules and Regulations' (12 May 2005), 12; cf. art 12, UNCITRAL Arbitration Rules (16 December 2013) UN Doc A/Res/31/98; IBA Guidelines 2014: General Standard 2. See also more generally Giorgetti et al 2020.

111 *Suez v Argentina* (Decision on Annulment) ICSID Case No ARB/03/17 (2018, McRae P, Jones & Abraham) at [171], where the Committee noted 'the generally unsatisfactory nature of the process for dealing with challenges to arbitrators', and the difficulty in 'formulating the appropriate test for deciding on disqualification in the absence of clear guidance in the Convention'. The Committee also contemplated at [172] a possible difference between commercial arbitration and investment arbitration in relation to the *perception* of lack of independence or impartiality, where in investment arbitration there is much greater a degree of public interest; see also Luttrell 2016.

112 Crawford 2015: 598.

113 IBA Guidelines 2014: Explanation to General Standard 3(c).

151 Since the resolution was adopted, the Secretariats of UNCITRAL and ICSID have published a draft Code of Conduct for Adjudicators in Investor–State Dispute Settlement.[114] Article 4(1) provides that: 'Adjudicators shall at all times be independent and impartial.'[115]

152 The Eighteenth Commission considered whether to include a specific provision on multiple roles (so-called double-hatting).[116] The *Institut* had already, in its Tokyo Resolution, decided that: 'Acceptance by individuals of different roles as counsel, arbitrators, members of ICSID *ad hoc* committees must not be allowed to affect the impartiality and independence of arbitrators.'[117] Returning to the issue in 2019, the Rapporteur noted that the issue was on the agenda at UNCITRAL; that there may be scope for a more absolute rule, but that this would raise a wide range of issues (in particular, concerning the diversity of appointments) that would go beyond the specific mandate of the Commission. He concluded that no further specific provision on multiple roles should be included in the draft resolution.[118]

2 *The Method for Determination of Challenges to Impartiality*

153 The challenge procedure under Article 58 of the ICSID Convention provides that, in the case of a challenge to one arbitrator of a three-person tribunal, the question is first to be referred to the other two Members of the Tribunal. Only if the two Members cannot agree does the Convention provide for a reference to the Chairman of the Administrative Council. This process has been criticised as failing to provide sufficient independence in the making of the disqualification decision.

154 By contrast, the UNCITRAL Rules provide that a challenge to an arbitrator will, if not otherwise accepted, be referred for decision to the appointing authority.[119]

155 There is some recent treaty practice pursuant to which States have explored other methods for the resolution of challenges. For example, Article 8.30(2) of CETA provides for challenges to a Member of the Tribunal to be referred to the President of the International Court of Justice for decision.[120]

156 In its proposals for revision of the ICSID Rules, the ICSID Secretariat proposes that the ability of the remaining members of the Tribunal to refer a challenge to the

114 ICSID/UNCITRAL 2020.

115 Ibid, 9.

116 Proposal of M Kohen (2019) 79 *Annuaire* 600.

117 Institut de Droit International 2013: Art 8.

118 (2019) 79 *Annuaire* 604. At the time of writing, this issue has not been resolved in the UNCITRAL/ICSID draft Code. Article 6 'Limit on Multiple Roles' remains in square brackets. For discussion of the issues, see ICSID/UNCITRAL 2020: [65]–[73].

119 Art 13(4), UNCITRAL Rules. Under art 6(2), in the absence of agreement between the Parties, the Secretary-General of the PCA designates the Appointing Authority.

120 The ICSID/UNCITRAL draft Code of Conduct does not deal with challenge procedures, providing only in art 12(2) that: 'The disqualification and removal procedures in the applicable rules shall continue to apply.'

Secretary-General for decision under Article 58 of the Convention be capable of exercise 'for any reason'.[121] The Working Paper notes that 'the Centre received numerous comments from States and the public that favoured repeal of the portion of Article 58 of the Convention conferring a decision on a challenge to co-arbitrators unless they are equally divided'.[122] This would require an amendment to the Convention itself and could not be achieved by a rule amendment. The rule amendment that is proposed simply clarifies that the remaining members of the tribunal need not be divided on the merits of the challenge.[123]

By paragraph (4), the *Institut* takes the view that challenges to the impartiality of a member **157**
of an arbitral tribunal 'should be determined by an independent third party decision-maker external to the tribunal'. By paragraph (5), it encourages Member States of the ICSID Convention to amend Article 58 so as to provide for an external determination of challenge applications.

Impartiality is alike an indispensible requirement for the members of any permanent **158**
international tribunal. It has been an important feature of the proposals for the establishment of a permanent Multilateral Investment Tribunal.[124] The assumption of full-time judicial office may nevertheless give rise to distinct considerations. The applicable Principles in this context were the subject of detailed consideration by a Study Group of the International Law Association, which adopted the Burgh House Principles on the Independence of the International Judiciary in 2004.[125]

121 ICSID 2020b: 301, Draft Arbitration Rule 23(2)(a).
122 ICSID 2018a: [333].
123 Ibid, [336].
124 EU Council 2018: [11]; UNCITRAL 2019b, UN Doc A/CN.9/WG.III/WP.167.
125 ILA 2005.

ARTICLE 4:

Composition

(1) **The composition of a tribunal shall be determined through a process of appointment that ensures that the parties to any dispute heard by that tribunal are treated with equality.**

(2) **This is so whether the tribunal is constituted as an arbitral tribunal or is established as a permanent tribunal. The composition of both kinds of tribunal must respect the equality of the parties; but the different legal character of arbitration and a permanent judicial body dictate a different application of the principle in each case:**

  (a) **The resolution of investment disputes by an arbitral tribunal composed of members appointed equally by the parties, with the president appointed by agreement (or, failing agreement, designated by an appointing authority) respects the principle of the equality of the parties, provided also that each member meets the same requirements of impartiality.**

  (b) **In the case of a permanent tribunal, the principle of the equality of the parties does not require that each party retain the ability to appoint a judge. The overriding consideration is the independence and impartiality of the members of the tribunal.**

(3) **A permanent tribunal of universal scope should comprise a body of independent judges of recognized competence in international law that equitably represents the principal legal systems of the world, elected through a transparent process.**

(4) **In the resolution of a specific dispute within the framework of a permanent tribunal, in order to respect the equality principle the rules governing the composition of a Bench or Chamber should either:**

  (a) **Exclude judges having the nationality of either the State party to the dispute or of the home State of the foreign investor; *or*,**

  (b) **Ensure that both such States have an equal opportunity to appoint a judge, if necessary by making provision for the appointment of a judge *ad hoc*.**

159 Article 4 addresses the role of the equality of the parties in the composition of the tribunal. In this instance, it has proved necessary to distinguish the position of arbitral tribunals from a permanent tribunal, in view of their respective different characters:

(1) paragraph (1) establishes the general principle – applicable in all cases – that the process of appointment must ensure that the parties to any dispute are treated with equality;

(2) paragraph (2) applies this principle, distinguishing between (a) the position of appointments to an arbitral tribunal and (b) the composition of a permanent tribunal;

(3) paragraphs (3) and (4) address the considerations applicable to the composition of a permanent tribunal and its Bench or Chamber constituted to decide a specific dispute.

Any system for the appointment of members to a tribunal for the resolution of disputes between investors and States must, in the interests of the parties and in the view of the wider public interests that are engaged in such cases, be demonstrably impartial. This is a basic condition for the legitimacy of any system for the binding determination of disputes according to law, as much applicable to the resolution of international investment disputes as any other. **160**

Equality as an attribute of the universally recognised right to a fair trial does not include, as an essential component, a right to appoint members of the tribunal. This is not a requirement of standing courts and tribunals, whether at the national or at the international level.[126] The claim that, of its nature, a move from party appointment to a standing tribunal 'may undermine the very foundations of arbitration (and of justice): the equality of arms between the parties'[127] is an overstatement, though it does serve to highlight an important difference between the resolution of such disputes by an arbitral tribunal established *ad hoc* by the parties and by a standing court or tribunal. The issue is one of the proper design of the constitution of such a tribunal, not the fact of its creation. **161**

This Commentary considers: **162**

(1) the appointment of arbitrators;
(2) the comparison between arbitral and permanent tribunals; and
(3) party appointments in permanent tribunals.

1 Appointment of Arbitrators

Equality of appointment is commonly cited as an important advantage of arbitration as contrasted with adjudication.[128] It holds in balance two inter-linked principles: party autonomy and the equality of the parties: the parties are free to choose their arbitrators, but they must be accorded equality in so doing. The most common method of giving effect to these two principles is for the tribunal to be constituted by arbitrators appointed by the parties in equal number, with a presiding arbitrator who is jointly appointed. **163**

Article 37(2)(b) of the ICSID Convention provides that, save where the parties otherwise agree, 'the Tribunal shall consist of three arbitrators, one arbitrator appointed by each party **164**

126 But cf. art 31, ICJ Statute, providing for the appointment of a judge *ad hoc* in cases in which the Bench does not include a judge of the nationality of the disputing State.
127 EFILA 2015: [5.4].
128 Born 2014: 1640.

and the third, who shall be the president of the Tribunal, appointed by agreement of the parties'.[129]

165 In this situation, each party has an equal and generally unfettered right to nominate its own arbitrator (subject only to the right of the other party to propose disqualification under Article 57 for a 'manifest lack of the qualities' required for his or her appointment). They also each have an equal right to participate in reaching agreement on the presiding arbitrator. These rules are subject to the autonomy of the parties, acting together, to agree an alternative form or method of composition of the Tribunal. The Convention also ensures that one party cannot frustrate the constitution of the Tribunal by refusing to appoint an arbitrator by conferring default powers on the Chairman of the Centre's Board.[130] The autonomy of the parties is otherwise limited only by the requirement that the number of arbitrators must be uneven[131] and by restrictions on the nationality of the arbitrators in order to ensure that (save where the parties agree) a majority of the Tribunal is not formed of arbitrators that are nationals of the host State.[132]

166 Article 38 adds that arbitrators appointed by the Chairman of the Administrative Council 'shall not be nationals of the Contracting State party to the dispute or of the Contracting State whose national is a party to the dispute'.

2 *Comparison between Arbitral and Permanent Tribunals*

167 If the parties are to have a role in the appointment of a particular tribunal to decide their case, such a role must be exercised in accordance with equality. But the question of constitutional principle is whether the observance of party appointment might, as those who favour reform argue, imperil the impartiality of the tribunal[133] or alternatively whether, as those who support the current system submit, party appointment is important to ensure equality of participation by both investors and States in the system.[134]

168 Ensuring impartiality in the design of a system for the settlement of investment disputes requires consideration of both forms of dispute resolution. It is not a matter of making a once-and-for-all binary choice between them.

169 The ICSID Convention (and the very widespread voluntary adoption by States of investor–State arbitration pursuant to investment treaties) were themselves in part a reaction to perceived shortcomings in other means of dispute settlement, including resort to diplomatic protection as a means of protecting foreign investment. The ICSID Convention has very wide acceptance by the majority of States, which is itself a strong indication of States'

129 The procedural implementation is set forth in ICSID Arbitration Rules 2–4.
130 Art 38, ICSID Convention.
131 Art 37(2)(a).
132 Art 39.
133 EC and Government of Canada 2017.
134 Bernadini 2017; Kho et al 2017.

acceptance in principle of the method for the settlement of investment disputes that the Convention offers. States may always choose to reform this mechanism by agreement, whether within the framework of the Convention or by subsequent separate agreement.

The adoption of the Dispute Settlement Understanding (DSU) in the World Trade Organization (WTO) in 1994 illustrates the capacity of States in a cognate field of international law to decide to move from a system more akin to arbitration to one that includes more institutional elements.[135] The DSU provides for a first instance system of *ad hoc* panels constituted on the proposal of the Secretariat (and *excluding* citizens of the disputing States unless the parties otherwise agree), but admitting the right of a disputing party to oppose a proposed appointment for compelling reasons.[136] The Appellate Body is, by contrast, a standing tribunal.[137] **170**

Arbitration is, of its nature, a form of dispute resolution to which parties choose to resort as an alternative to other forms of dispute resolution. Resort to arbitration always depends upon the consent of the parties. This is, as the Directors of the World Bank observed at the outset, 'the cornerstone of the jurisdiction of the Centre'.[138] It is only where the parties have so given their consent that the Convention excludes any other remedy.[139] The Convention does not seek to supplant other mechanisms for the resolution of investment disputes, whether at the national or the international level, save where such consent has been given. Such mechanisms may either continue to exist (as in the case of diplomatic protection) or be created in parallel with arbitration. **171**

International law does not generally prescribe a single method for the resolution of disputes. Rather, it encourages States to resort to a range of different methods for the pacific settlement of disputes, including 'negotiation, enquiry, mediation, conciliation, arbitration, judicial settlement . . . or other peaceful means of their own choice'.[140] After the establishment of the Permanent Court of Justice, States continued to maintain in force the 1899 and 1907 Hague Conventions establishing the Permanent Court of Arbitration (PCA),[141] under whose aegis States and private parties now frequently consent to submit disputes to arbitration rather than litigation. **172**

Party appointment is not an invariable element of all systems of arbitration. There are currently a number of prominent examples of international arbitral systems that provide for institutional appointment of arbitrators.[142] The question of whether party or institutional **173**

135 Dispute Settlement Understanding (signed 15 April 1994) 1869 UNTS 401, Annex 2 to Marrakesh Agreement establishing the World Trade Organization 1868 UNTS 186.

136 Art 8, ibid.

137 Art 17, ibid.

138 ICSID 1965: [23].

139 Art 26, ICSID Convention.

140 Art 33, Charter of the United Nations (signed 26 June 1945, entered into force 24 October 1945) 59 Stat 1031.

141 Convention for the Pacific Settlement of International Disputes (signed 29 July 1899) 187 Con TS 410; Convention for the Pacific Settlement of International Disputes (signed 18 October 1907).

142 Kaufmann-Kohler and Potestà give the examples of the Court of Arbitration for Sport and other sporting arbitral bodies: Geneva CIDS (Kaufmann-Kohler and Potestà) 2016: [96].

appointment of arbitrators is preferable in international commercial arbitration has also been recently debated.[143]

174 The process of appointment or election of judges to standing international courts and tribunals has itself raised difficult challenges, a matter considered by the *Institut* in its work on the position of the international judge.[144] In view of the indispensable security of tenure of an international judge, appointments to a standing court or tribunal have of their nature longer-term effects.

175 The particular issues that have arisen in weighing the comparative advantages of each system of dispute resolution in light of the method of appointment include:

(1) whether enabling parties to individually choose their arbitrators can affect the objectivity of the decision-making process, if it encourages each party to appoint individuals who are sympathetic to their position, a selection process that has the potential to give rise to a moral hazard or to lead to the dependence of particular arbitrators on particular appointing parties or categories of parties (whether investors or States);[145]
(2) whether, conversely, a system of party appointment promotes legitimacy through ensuring that both the private party claimant and the State have an equal stake in the constitution of the tribunal that will decide their dispute, which in turn promotes engagement and compliance;
(3) if a standing tribunal is established, how to ensure that the selection process for its members is impartial; in particular, if all the tribunal members are appointed by States, how to ensure that it does not or is not perceived by its composition as institutionally favouring States; and whether that risk, if it exists, could be mitigated by the incorporation into the system of some involvement of groups representing the investment community.[146]

176 Debate on this issue in the Eighteenth Commission recognised that what was involved was essentially a policy choice between the respective advantages and disadvantages of two different types of dispute settlement, which would have to be taken by States in the design and provision of available mechanisms for the resolution of investment disputes. In view of the considerations outlined above, even if a permanent international tribunal is established, it is unlikely that such a tribunal will wholly exclude the incidence of arbitration. Since both mechanisms are recognised in international law as available for the resolution of international disputes, the members of the Commission considered that the most useful role for the *Institut* would be to consider the implications of the equality principle in both arbitral and permanent tribunals.

143 Paulsson 2013: 162; cf. Brower and Rosenberg 2013.
144 Institut de Droit International 2011: 124; see also Mackenzie et al 2010.
145 Bonnitcha et al 2017; EC and Government of Canada 2017: [11].
146 UNCITRAL Report 2017a: [36].

Members of the Commission considered that, despite the challenges, party appointment of arbitrators is one of the main features that distinguishes arbitration from litigation. They concluded that the importance attached to party autonomy in arbitration justifies retention of this feature, provided that impartiality of arbitrators is ensured.[147] 177

The *Institut* concluded in paragraph (2)(a) that: 'The resolution of investment disputes by an arbitral tribunal composed of members appointed equally by the parties, with the president appointed by agreement (or, failing agreement, designated by an appointing authority) respects the principle of the equality of the parties, provided also that each member meets the same requirements of impartiality.' 178

3 *Election and Appointment in Permanent Tribunals*

The implications for the equality of the parties of a transition from an arbitration model to a permanent tribunal are developed in the second report of the Geneva Center for International Dispute Settlement: 179

> Transitioning from an *ad hoc* system that allows virtually complete control over composition by the disputing parties to a permanent or semi-permanent system necessarily reduces the role for disputing parties and conversely increases that of the treaty parties ... Such dilution of powers concerns all disputing parties, including respondent States who lose the 'right' to influence the composition of the body as disputing parties. However, in practice, it will be perceived as affecting the investor-party more heavily, as States will be able to contribute to the composition of the body in their capacity as treaty parties. In other words, in an asymmetric setting such as investor–State dispute settlement, the shift from an *ad hoc* to a permanent setting means that one category of disputing parties loses control over the selection process, which remains entirely in the hands of the other because the latter is at the same time a treaty party.[148]

Nevertheless, a number of permanent or standing tribunals also allow a role for party appointment. One of the reasons for such a provision is to ensure the equality of the parties in the resolution of specific disputes. 180

The *International Court of Justice* itself, though a permanent court, also incorporates an element of party appointment within its procedure: 181

(1) judges of the nationality of each of the parties retain their right to sit in the case before the Court; and

[147] (2019) 79 *Annuaire* 563 (Alexandrov), 564 (Boisson de Chazournes, d'Argent), 565 (Giardina, Kazazi, Kohen), 566 (Mikulka, Reinisch), 567 (Stern, Treves, Vinuesa).

[148] Geneva CIDS 2017: [14].

(2) if the Court does not include on its Bench a judge of the nationality of one or both of the disputing parties, that party may choose a person to sit on the Court as a judge *ad hoc*.[149]

182 Every judge must make the same declaration 'that he will exercise his powers impartially and conscientiously'.[150] Judges *ad hoc* 'shall take part in the decision in complete equality with their colleagues'.[151]

183 The addition of this provision was considered important in the framing of the Statute so as to maintain a balance between States' confidence and participation in the system, while at the same time ensuring the equality of the parties. It would have been possible to secure equality by excluding any judge of the same nationality as either party, but only at the expense of confidence and participation.[152] Lord Phillimore observed: '[I]t would be preferable to give a national representative to both parties, not only to protect their interests but to enable the Court to understand certain questions which require highly specialised knowledge and relate to the differences between the various legal systems.'[153] Far from becoming obsolete, the institution of the judge *ad hoc* has proved to be an enduring feature of the Court's procedure.[154]

184 The appointment of national judges may be found in standing bilateral tribunals in the investment field:

(1) The *Iran–US Claims Tribunal* provides the most direct example of an existing standing international tribunal to resolve investor–State claims, albeit that it applies only as between two States. It consists of nine members: three appointed by each of the States, while the remaining three members (including the President) are to be selected by agreement between the States.[155] Absent agreement, the default provisions of the UNCITRAL Rules apply, with the effect that the Secretary-General of the Permanent

149 Art 31, ICJ Statute.

150 Art 17(2).

151 Art 31(6).

152 [31.1] (Kooijmans) in Zimermann et al 2012: 531–2.

153 Advisory Committee of Jurists, *Procès Verbaux* (1920), 528–9. For cogent early criticism of this aspect of the procedure of the PCIJ, see Lauterpacht 1933: 236–44.

154 Schwebel 1999. The *Institut* considered the question in 1954 within the framework of the 22nd Commission (Rapporteur: Huber): (1954) 45 *Annuaire* vol I, 407 at 427–30, session: vol II at 84–90. The Members of the Commission were divided on whether to recommend the retention or abolition of the institution of the judge *ad hoc*. The Report acknowledged (at 429) that 'l'idée de la parité ou égalité totale des parties au litige a une grande force psychologique. L'introduction du juge *ad hoc* s'explique donc très naturellement ainsi que les fortes résistances probables contre l'abolition de ce système.' The Resolution (vol II, 296 at 298) recommended in art 5 that: 'If the system of *ad hoc* judges cannot be abandoned, it is as a minimum highly desirable that the appointment of such judges should be subject to guarantees as nearly as possible equivalent to those governing the election of titular judges.'

155 Art III(1), Declaration of the Democratic and Popular Government of Algeria concerning the Settlement of Claims by the Government of the United States of America and the Government of the Islamic Republic of Iran ('Claims Settlement Declaration') 19 January 1981 (1983) 1 Iran–US CTR 9.

Court of Arbitration (PCA) may designate an Appointing Authority.[156] The provisions for the appointment of members to a three-member tribunal are to like effect.[157]

(2) The *CETA* Tribunal follows a similar approach. It is also to be constituted on the basis of nationals drawn equally from Canada and the European Union (five members from each), with five further members required to be nationals of third States.[158] The members are all to be designated by the CETA Joint Committee, an executive body comprising representatives of Canada and the European Union.[159] The President of the Tribunal must be a national of a third State.[160] The provisions of the final text of the EU–Vietnam Investment Protection Agreement are to like effect, save that the three-way division of members is, like the Iran–US Claims Tribunal, limited to three members in each category rather than five.[161]

Some regional human rights courts adopt a solution similar to that of the International Court of Justice: **185**

(1) The *European Convention on Human Rights* also provides that judges appointed by the Contracting State concerned in the case are entitled to sit in any Chamber or Grand Chamber constituted to hear the matter. If there is none, the President of the Court shall appoint a judge *ad hoc*.[162]
(2) The Pact of San José establishing the *Inter-American Court of Human Rights* contains similar provisions ensuring the representation on the Court of judges of the State engaged in the case.[163]

By contrast, the Protocol establishing the African Court of Human Rights does not contemplate that all Member States shall have a judge of their nationality on the Court. On the contrary, Article 22 provides that: 'If a judge is a national of any State which is a party to a case submitted to the Court, that judge shall not hear the case.'[164] **186**

A key objective of the establishment of a specialised system for the resolution of international investment disputes has, from the outset, been – and continues to be – to depoliticise such disputes.[165] Any process for the appointment of judges to a permanent tribunal **187**

156 Art III(2), Claims Settlement Declaration.
157 Art 7, Iran–US CTR.
158 Art 8.27(2), CETA.
159 Art 26(1).
160 Art 8.27(8).
161 Art 3.38(2), Final text of EU–Vietnam Investment Protection Agreement.
162 Art 26, Convention for the Protection of Human Rights and Fundamental Freedoms (signed 4 November 1950, entered into force 3 September 1953) 213 UNTS 222, as amended.
163 Art 55, American Convention on Human Rights, 'Pact of San José, Costa Rica' (signed 22 November 1969, entered into force 18 July 1978) 1144 UNTS 123.
164 Art 22, Protocol to the African Charter on Human and Peoples' Rights on the Establishment of an African Court on Human and Peoples' Rights (adopted 10 June 1998, entered into force 25 January 2004).
165 Broches 1972: 344; UNCITRAL Report 2017a: [9].

would, to be legitimate, have to address how to ensure that such a process did not itself become politicised.[166] Such a process is as susceptible of giving rise to equality and impartiality concerns as appointment to individual arbitral tribunals if it were to lack integrity. Indeed, the problem of ensuring that the parties retain confidence in the impartiality of the tribunal is likely, as Lauterpacht observed as long ago as 1933, to arise principally in the context of a permanent tribunal with a fixed body of judges, for the very reason that the parties cannot play an equal role in its constitution.[167]

188 It might be possible to address this asymmetry through the design of a permanent tribunal that included a specific role in the election or appointment process for the investment community. However, the great majority of the members of the Commission[168] did not favour this course on a number of grounds:

(1) A permanent tribunal would constitute an exercise of public authority, whose members ought themselves to be appointed by public authorities.
(2) Regional human rights courts (and national constitutional courts) have shown themselves capable of determining cases in favour of individual claimants, despite being comprised of judges appointed only by States.
(3) The investment community is not homogeneous and does not speak with one voice. It is not clear who would be entitled to represent it in this process.
(4) If the appointment of judges were to involve interests beyond those of the States, it is not clear why this should be limited to investors, since there are other groups in civil society that also claim to represent other interests in the determination of investment disputes.

189 On the other hand, a key element in the design of a permanent tribunal will be how it ensures appropriate diversity of its members. There are many dimensions of this issue that go beyond the remit of this resolution, which is focused on the equality of the parties.[169]

190 In light of the nature of investment disputes, it would seem necessary for the power of appointment of any permanent tribunal to reflect fairly the perspectives of capital-exporting and capital-importing States. These categories are not fixed. Many States both export and import capital. This balance may, in the case of particular States, change over time. But a power of appointment to a tribunal that was perceived as too heavily weighted in one direction or the other might well affect the extent to which the tribunal was perceived as fully capable of respecting the equality of the

[166] Geneva CIDS 2017; Geneva CIDS (Kaufmann-Kohler and Potestà) 2016: [167]; UNCITRAL Report 2017a: [34].

[167] Lauterpacht 1933: 236. As noted above, Lauterpacht did not consider that the inclusion of judges *ad hoc* provided any solution to this problem. On the contrary, he deprecated such a solution as likely to imperil the impartiality of the tribunal.

[168] Note, however, the comment of Boisson de Chazournes at (2019) 79 *Annuaire* 54: 'It is therefore necessary to involve non-state parties in the establishment of a standing tribunal if its attractiveness is to be maintained.'

[169] Geneva CIDS 2017: Pt III B 3, discussing diversity, in general and including geographical diversity and gender diversity.

parties.[170] However, in part in view of the difficult questions of definition that would arise, the Eighteenth Commission did not consider that it was appropriate to single out this factor from the range of other considerations of equitable composition that would have to be balanced in any appointment or election process.[171]

The Commission concluded, in light of the above research, that in the case of a permanent tribunal of universal scope, it was necessary to distinguish between the election of members to the body as a whole, which is dealt with in paragraph (4), and the composition of the Bench or Chamber constituted to hear a particular dispute in paragraph (5). **191**

In electing the tribunal as a whole, it would suffice to provide for 'a body of independent judges of recognized competence in international law that equitably represents the principal legal systems of the world, elected through a transparent process'. **192**

When a Bench or Chamber is appointed to hear a particular dispute, on the other hand, the nationality of the individual members of the Bench may become a particular consideration. The equality principle would preclude the constitution of a Bench that included a judge of the nationality of only one of the parties. Here, comparative reference to the constitution of other international courts provides two alternative models by way of response: **193**

(1) a provision to ensure that a judge of the nationality of (or appointed by) each Party must sit on the Bench (ICJ, European Court of Human Rights [ECtHR], Inter-American Court of Human Rights [IACtHR], Iran–US Claims Tribunal [IUSCT]); or
(2) the exclusion of a judge of either nationality from the Bench (WTO, African Court of Human and Peoples' Rights [ACtHR]).

The first model conceives the permanent tribunal as a hybrid that continues to import from arbitration an element of party appointment. The second conceives the permanent tribunal as fully detached from connections with either of the disputing parties. The choice between these two models involves wider considerations than the equality principle. It engages the question of the most appropriate conditions in the present state of international society for the submission of States to international adjudication. The Commission took the view that these considerations went beyond the scope of its work and that it would suffice to indicate that either alternative model would meet the requirements of the equality principle. This is reflected in paragraph (5). **194**

170 Ibid, [59].

171 A proposal to include such a requirement was made in draft art 4(3), the Rapporteur's first draft (2019) 79 *Annuaire* 595, but was abandoned following consultation with Commission members: ibid, 608.

C. Part Two: Application to the Procedure of the Tribunal

CHAPTER I: PARTIES

195 Part Two of the resolution is concerned with a set of issues relating to the application of the equality principle to the procedure of the Tribunal. It consists of three Chapters: (1) Parties; (2) Pleading and Evidence; and (3) Substantive Equality of Arms.

196 Chapter 1 considers the application of the equality principle to three elements affecting the parties to an investment claim. Article 5 considers the position of multiple claimants. Article 6 addresses counterclaims. Article 7 concerns third-person submissions.

ARTICLE 5:
Multiple Claimants

(1) **Where several investors seek to institute their claims in a single arbitral proceeding against the same State, the tribunal shall ensure, in its determination of jurisdiction and admissibility and in its procedural directions, that the parties are treated with equality.**

(2) **When determining its jurisdiction, the tribunal must be satisfied that:**

(a) **Each claimant individually satisfies the jurisdictional requirements (both of the instrument of consent and, where applicable, Article 25 of the ICSID Convention) in order to bring its claim; and**

(b) **The claim as a whole advances a single dispute, in that the interest represented by the claimants is in all respects identical, so that the respondent is not prejudiced by having to defend itself against claims that differ materially in the interest to be vindicated.**

The tribunal may hold a claim brought by multiple claimants to be inadmissible if it finds that the manner in which the claim is brought would adversely affect the tribunal's ability to ensure that both sides of the dispute are treated with equality in the presentation of their case or in their defence of the claims.

Article 5 addresses the application of the equality principle in cases where there are **197**
multiple claimants. The Eighteenth Commission preferred the terminology of multiple claimants over 'mass claims', because the latter expression is not a term of art in investment arbitration, which contains no special provisions for representative or class actions.[172] This question has arisen, in particular in, cases of multiple claimants bringing joint suit on similar but distinct legal instruments.[173]

As to date, large multiparty claims have not proceeded to a final resolution, 'the complex- **198**
ities of a mass claim case and the various solutions proposed for it have not been tested in practice'.[174] Whether the number of claimants poses insurmountable problems for the management of a case involves balancing the claimants' right to be heard and the respondent's due process rights, as well as the capacity of the arbitral framework to manage the claim process.[175]

172 *Adamakopoulos v Cyprus* (Decision on Jurisdiction) ICSID Case No ARB/15/49 (2020, McRae P, Escobar & Kohen), [190]. See generally ICSID Secretariat 2018: vol 3, Sch 7, Pt II. ICSID does not propose specific rules to deal with multiple claimants.

173 *Abaclat v Argentina* (Decision on Jurisdiction and Admissibility) ICSID Case No ARB/07/5, IIC 504 (2011, Tercier P, van den Berg & Abi-Saab (dissenting)); *Ambiente Ufficio SpA v Argentina* (Decision on Jurisdiction and Admissibility) ICSID Case No ARB/08/09, IIC 576 (2013, Simma P, Böckstiegel & Torres Bernárdez (dissenting)); *Alemanni v Argentina* (Decision on Jurisdiction and Admissibility) ICSID Case No ARB/07/8, IIC 666 (2014, Berman P, Böckstiegel & Thomas (concurring)).

174 *Adamakopoulos* (Decision on Jurisdiction), [189]. See also Szczudlik 2018: 198–213.

175 *Adamakopoulos* (Decision on Jurisdiction), [224].

199 In such a situation, the claims of each claimant remain distinct and the Tribunal must satisfy itself as to jurisdiction and the merits of each claimant's claim.[176] Accordingly, Article 5(2)(a) requires first that each claimant individually satisfy the jurisdictional requirements in order to bring its claims.

200 But the question remains: what are the limits, if any, on the aggregation of such claims in a single proceeding?[177] To what extent may the number of claimants disturb the equilibrium between the parties, depriving the respondent State of its ability to defend itself?

201 One approach would be to require evidence of secondary consent to multi-party arbitration.[178] This approach has been adopted (by majority) in US Supreme Court decisions that limit the aggregation of claims into class action arbitrations in consumer cases.[179] Such an approach may lead to unnecessarily fragmented proceedings and potentially a denial of justice for individual claimants.[180] The majority of a recent Tribunal did not accept 'the argument that a separate consent to mass claims would be required over and above the consent given by a state to the jurisdiction of an investment tribunal when it became party to the BIT'.[181]

202 Article 25(1) of the ICSID Convention requires the existence of a 'legal dispute arising directly out of an investment, between a Contracting State . . . and a national of another Contracting State'. This test contemplates a *single dispute*.[182] While it is possible that such a dispute may involve more than one party on each side, 'the interest represented on each side of the dispute has to be in all essential respects identical for all of those involved on that side of the dispute'.[183] The Tribunal considered that this required the claimants to adduce sufficient evidence to enable it to determine whether there was in substance a single dispute.[184]

203 The Eighteenth Commission considered that this test of identity of interest supplies the most appropriate basis on which to ensure that the respondent is not prejudiced by having to defend itself against claims that differ materially in the interest to be vindicated. This is a distinct concept, of wider reach to that of identity of parties, because it focuses on the substantive character of the legal interest that the respective claimants have in common. It enables the efficient aggregation of claims, while at the same time maintaining the equality of the parties. This is the test that is adopted in Article 5(2)(b) as the requirement for the

176 van Houtte and McAsey 2012; *Ambiente*, [114]–[122].

177 See *Adamakopoulos* (Decision on Jurisdiction), [205], where the majority of the Tribunal did not 'accept that on the basis of claims involving a relatively small number of claimants it is possible to conclude that jurisdiction over a mass claim of 956 claimants is generally accepted in ICSID arbitration'.

178 *Abaclat* (Abi-Saab dissent) [146]–[175]; *Ambiente* (Torres Bernárdez dissent) [99]–[105].

179 *Abaclat* (Abi-Saab dissent) [150]–[152], citing *Stolt-Nielsen SA v Animal Feeds International Corporation* 130 S Ct 1758 (2010); *AT&T Mobility LLC v Conception* 131 S Ct 1740 (2011).

180 Born 2011. For a detailed study of the issues, see Strong 2013.

181 *Adamakopoulos* (Decision on Jurisdiction), [201].

182 Ibid, [209]: 'The question, following the approach of *Alemanni*, is whether the claims can be regarded as a single dispute.'

183 *Alemanni*, [292].

184 Ibid, [294].

joinder of multiple claimants into a single proceeding, in addition to the requirement under Article 5(2)(a) that each claimant have a proper basis to invoke the jurisdiction of the tribunal.

Even where such a requirement is met, an international investment tribunal hearing the claim of multiple claimants against a single respondent must still be astute to ensure that its processes ensure equality of arms, since, as one Tribunal observed: **204**

> [I]f it did find that the inherent circumstances of the case stood in the way of preserving the equality between the Parties or risked denying either one side or the other a full and ample opportunity to present its case, then it would have to give serious consideration to whether it could allow the arbitration to proceed, or to proceed in its present form. This is because – and quite irrespective of the fact that Article 52 of the ICSID Convention specifically includes 'a serious departure from a fundamental rule of procedure' among the grounds for annulment – both the principle of equality of arms and the right to be heard are fundamental to the judicial process.[185]

For this reason, paragraph (2) adds by way of proviso that, even if the application of the two-part test set out above would result in a determination that the tribunal has jurisdiction over a claim of multiple claimants, a claim may still be held to be inadmissible if 'the manner in which the claim is brought would adversely affect the tribunal's ability to ensure that both sides of the dispute are treated with equality in the presentation of their case or in their defence of the claims'. **205**

[185] *Alemanni* (2014, Berman P, Böckstiegel & Thomas (concurring)), [323].

ARTICLE 6:

Counterclaims

(1) **The ability of a respondent to assert a counterclaim that is admissible before a tribunal ensures the procedural equality of the parties.**

(2) **In order to be admissible, such a counterclaim must:**

(a) **Be within the jurisdiction of the tribunal; and,**

(b) **Arise directly out of the subject matter of the investment.**

(3) **The jurisdictional requirement is met when, by virtue of the instrument of consent invoked by the respondent, the tribunal would have had jurisdiction over the counterclaim had it been asserted as a primary claim. Whether or not the tribunal has jurisdiction over a counterclaim does not depend upon the respondent invoking the same ground of jurisdiction as that relied upon by the claimant for its claim, nor is the tribunal's jurisdiction limited by the scope of the dispute as framed by the claimant in its Request for Arbitration.**

(4) **Where the dispute is submitted to arbitration under the ICSID Convention, the requirement in Article 46 that the counterclaim must also be 'otherwise within the jurisdiction of the Centre' means that it must fall within the criteria of Article 25(1) of the Convention by being a 'legal dispute arising directly out of an investment, between a Contracting State ... and a national of another Contracting State.'**

(5) **The requirement of sufficiency of connection with the subject matter of the dispute is met where the counterclaim concerns the same investment that gave rise to the claim. It does not require that the counterclaim be founded upon the same legal instrument or cause of action asserted by the claimant.**

(6) **The tribunal may find a counterclaim to be admissible, whether it is founded upon international law or host State law, provided that it fulfils the other requirements set out in this Article and concerns a subject matter that is capable of submission to arbitration.**

1 Context

206 The ability of a State against whom a claim has been brought to institute a counterclaim may serve the equality principle in both its procedural and its constitutional dimensions.

207 Procedural equality is served by the availability of a right to counterclaim. By allowing the respondent to raise its counter complaints in the same proceeding, the tribunal ensures that it gives even-handed consideration to the respective claims of both parties arising out of the same dispute. At the same time, procedural equality requires a close connection between claim and counterclaim. If the respondent were able to pursue claims that were unconnected with the claim, the counterclaim procedure may become an instrument by which valid claims could be suppressed and consent disregarded. The institution of the counterclaim also serves other purposes connected to the good administration of justice. It promotes judicial efficiency and avoids excessive adjudicatory fragmentation by ensuring that closely related claims brought by the respective parties can be adjudicated within the framework of the same proceeding on the same evidentiary basis.

The counterclaim can also be said to promote equality of the parties in its constitutional aspect. International investment tribunals are established in order to provide a neutral forum in which the claims of investors against host States can be determined. The ability of the State to assert a counterclaim rebalances the asymmetry that otherwise applies where the claimant is always an investor.[186] **208**

Yet, at the same time, the availability *vel non* of an international arbitral forum for the vindication of a State's counterclaim is not of itself indicative of a structural lack of balance within the system. The scope of the tribunal's jurisdiction is a result of the deliberate choices made by States in framing the arbitration agreements in investment treaties.[187] The State retains its remedies against the investor before national courts. Investment arbitration only substitutes for national adjudication to the extent that the parties consent, but not otherwise. The decision of a tribunal that it does not have jurisdiction over a counterclaim is not *per se* a denial of justice. It is a reflection of the limitations imposed upon its jurisdiction by the scope of the parties' agreement. **209**

Nevertheless, in view of its potentially valuable role in ensuring the equality of the parties, it is necessary to examine the extent to which the requirements for the institution of a counterclaim in investment arbitration have worked in practice to afford equality in the context of treaty disputes.[188] The point is significant in practical terms. Very few counterclaims in ICSID proceedings have succeeded.[189] Many have failed on preliminary objections as to jurisdiction and admissibility. The requisite conditions for jurisdiction and admissibility have given rise to controversy within the jurisprudence.[190] Yet, Article 46 of the Convention expressly provides for the availability of a right to counterclaim. It is one of the provisions that gives effect to the general consideration by the Executive Directors that, 'since the Convention permits the institution of proceedings by host States as well as **210**

186 Bubrowski 2013: 212; Toral and Schultz 2010: 577.

187 For example, the most recent multilateral investment treaty, the CPTPP, limits the availability of counterclaims to those connected to an investment agreement or licence and excludes this possibility in respect of claims of breach of treaty: art 9.19(2). This operation of this paragraph is currently suspended under art 2, as are the paragraphs providing for the corresponding claims under investment agreements and authorisations, until the Parties agree otherwise.

188 See generally: De Nanteuil 2018; Sharpe and Jacob 2018: 347.

189 For recent important exceptions, see: *Perenco Ecuador Ltd v Ecuador* (Interim Decision on the Environmental Counterclaim) ICSD Case No ARB/08/6 (2015, Tomka P, Kaplan & Thomas); *Burlington Resources Inc v Ecuador* (Decision on Counterclaims) ICSID Case No ARB/08/5 (2017, Kaufmann-Kohler P, Stern & Drymer), where the Parties consented to the Tribunal's jurisdiction over the counterclaim by *compromis*.

190 See, e.g., *Roussalis v Romania* (Award) ICSID Case No ARB/06/1 (2011, Hanotiau P, Giardina & Reisman (dissenting)); *Gavazzi v Romania* (Decision on Jurisdiction, Admissibility and Liability) ICSID Case No ARB/12/25 (2015, van Houtte P, Veeder & Rubino-Sammartano (dissenting)).

by investors . . . the provisions of the Convention should be equally adapted to the requirements of both cases'.[191]

211 Concern over the limited availability of counterclaims in investment arbitration is one of the issues that States have raised in UNCITRAL Working Group III on possible reform of investor–State dispute settlement. The UNCITRAL Secretariat has proposed that:

> The Working Group may wish to consider devising a framework in which States could raise counterclaims in ISDS, which would reduce uncertainty, promote fairness and rule of law, and ultimately ensure a balance between respondent States and claimant investors. Such a framework could also have a positive impact on the duration and cost of proceedings as well as on a number of other procedural issues.[192]

212 Recognising the central importance of the ability to pursue counterclaims for the equality of the parties, the Eighteenth Commission devoted close attention to the proper construction of the requirements of jurisdiction and admissibility.[193]

213 Article 46 of the ICSID Convention provides:

> Except as the parties otherwise agree, the Tribunal shall, if requested by a party, determine any incidental or additional claims or counterclaims arising directly out of the subject-matter of the dispute provided that they are within the scope of the consent of the parties and are otherwise within the jurisdiction of the Centre.

214 This formulation imposes three requirements for a counterclaim. It must be:

(1) 'within the scope of the consent of the parties'
(2) 'otherwise within the jurisdiction of the Centre'; and
(3) 'arising directly out of the subject-matter of the dispute'.

215 The first two of these elements go to jurisdiction. They both relate to essential elements of the jurisdictional requirements of the Convention in Article 25. The third element – connection with the subject matter – is not one of jurisdiction. It is not found in the part of the Convention that deals with jurisdiction, appearing instead in the section dealing with the powers and functions of the Tribunal. It is properly to be regarded as a requirement of admissibility:[194] the counterclaim that does not meet this requirement is not precluded from

191 ICSID 1965: [13].
192 UNCITRAL 2020c, UN Doc A/CN.9/WG.III/WP.193.
193 (2019) 79 *Annuaire* 568 (Alexandrov), 569 (Boisson de Chazournes, d'Argent), 570 (Gaja, Giardina), 571 (Kazazi, Kohen), 572 (Mikulka, Reinisch, Stern), 573 (Treves, Vinuesa), *contra* Crawford 544–5.
194 Schreuer et al 2009: 751.

being heard by the Centre; it simply cannot be entertained within the framework of the particular proceeding.[195]

Article 21(3) of the revised text of the UNCITRAL Rules 2010 provides that 'the respondent may make a counter-claim . . . provided that the arbitral tribunal has jurisdiction over it'. This revision was specifically intended to ensure that the counterclaim rule could apply equally to investment arbitration as to commercial arbitration.[196] The Commission left the test of sufficiency of connection for tribunals to determine on a case-by-case basis. **216**

Before the International Court of Justice, a counterclaim, in order to be admissible, must meet two requirements: (1) it must come within the jurisdiction of the Court; and (2) it must be 'directly connected with the subject-matter of the claim of the other party'.[197] The Court defines counterclaims as 'autonomous legal acts the object of which is to submit new claims to the Court which are, at the same time, linked to the principal claims, in so far as they are formulated as "counter" claims that react to those principal claims'.[198] **217**

Within the Eighteenth Commission, the draft article on counterclaims underwent significant revision from the Rapporteur's first draft.[199] Nevertheless, the Commission was able to present the final text as consensus draft. In plenary, Article 6(1) was amended to delete an earlier reference to counterclaims being an 'important assurance' of equality, and to provide instead simply that '[t]he ability of a respondent to assert a counterclaim that is admissible before a tribunal *ensures* the procedural equality of the parties'.[200] The provision did not otherwise provoke debate or amendment. It was adopted with 62 votes in favour, 3 votes against and 8 abstentions.[201] **218**

The resulting Article is a modest attempt to provide reasonable flexibility in the availability of counterclaims in order to ensure the equality of the parties, while at the same time respecting the general prerequisites of jurisdiction and admissibility. It seeks, in particular, to supply a framework for the consistent treatment of the admission of counterclaims by clarifying the connecting factors applicable to the determination of jurisdiction and admissibility in the specific context of investment arbitration. **219**

Article 6 opens in paragraph (1) by confirming that '[t]he ability of a respondent to assert a counterclaim that is admissible before a tribunal ensures the procedural equality of the parties'. It then divides its treatment of counterclaims into two parts, which are enumerated in paragraph (2): **220**

195 Atanansova et al 2014: 378–80.
196 UNCITRAL (Paulson and Petrochilos) 2006: [174].
197 Art 80, ICJ Rules of Court.
198 *Alleged Violations of Sovereign Rights and Maritime Spaces in the Caribbean Sea (Nicaragua v Colombia)* (Counterclaims Order of 15 November 2017) [2017] ICJ Rep 289, [18].
199 (2019) 79 *Annuaire* 594–5. A draft paragraph dealing with the types of compromissory clauses in investment treaties was deleted on the proposal of Kohen as outside the scope of the Commission: ibid, 601.
200 Emphasis added.
201 (2020) 80 *Annuaire* 48.

(1) *jurisdiction* – the requirement that the counterclaim be within the jurisdiction of the tribunal, which is treated more specifically in paragraphs (3) and (4); and
(2) *admissibility* – the requirement of sufficiency of connection, which it defines as arising 'directly out of the subject matter of the investment', a test that is further developed in paragraphs (5) and (6).

The requirements are cumulative. It is necessary to comment further on each of them.

2 *Jurisdiction*

221 *Paragraph (3)* concerns the scope of the jurisdiction *ratione materiae* conferred upon the tribunal over the counterclaim by virtue of the instrument of consent invoked by the respondent (both parties already being subject to the tribunal's jurisdiction *ratione personae* by virtue of their respective decisions to submit their claim or counterclaim as the case may be). It contains both a positive and a negative element:

(1) *positively*, it confirms that the test for the tribunal's subject-matter jurisdiction is to be determined by whether the tribunal 'would have had jurisdiction over the counterclaim had it been asserted as a primary claim'; and
(2) *negatively*, it provides that this 'does not depend upon the respondent invoking the same ground of jurisdiction as that relied upon by the claimant for its claim, nor . . . the scope of the dispute as framed by the claimant in its Request for Arbitration.'

222 This flows from the general principle that the agreement to arbitrate is autonomous and is separable from the substantive obligations to which it applies.[202]

223 Where the instrument of consent contains a general bilateral clause that refers to arbitration 'all disputes concerning an investment', then (subject to meeting the other requirements of Article 6) the tribunal may take jurisdiction over a counterclaim relating to that investment.[203]

224 So, in *Tethyan v Pakistan*,[204] the Tribunal interpreted a treaty clause that referred to 'dispute[s] between a Party and an investor of the other Party relating to an investment'

[202] *Elf Aquitaine Iran v National Iranian Oil Co* (Preliminary Award) XI YB Comm Arb 97 (14 January 1982), [256]; *Duke Energy International Peru Investments No 1 Ltd v Peru* (Decision on Annulment) ICSID Case No ARB/03/28 (2011, McLachlan P, Hascher & Tomka), [131].

[203] *SGS Société Générale de Surveillance SA v Philippines* (Decision on Jurisdiction) ICSID Case No ARB/02/6, 8 ICSID Rep 515 (2004, El-Kosheri P, Crawford & Crivellaro (dissenting)), [131]; *Saluka Investments BV v Czech Republic* (Decision on Jurisdiction over the Czech Republic's Counterclaim) UNCITRAL (2004, Watts C, Behrens & Fortier), [39]; *Goetz v Burundi* (Award) ICSID Case No ARB/01/2 (2012, Guillaume P, Bredin & El-Kosheri), [278]; Douglas 2009: Rule 26, [489]–[491].

[204] *Tethyan Copper Co Pty Ltd v Pakistan* (Decision on Jurisdiction and Liability) ICSID Case No ARB/12/1 (2017, Sachs P, Alexandrov & Lord Hoffmann).

and provided that 'either party to the dispute may . . . refer the dispute to [ICSID]'.[205] It held that:

> [N]ot only the language used in Article 13 itself, but also the expressed intention of the authors of the ICSID Convention not to provide for a '*one way street*' for investors, together with the absence of any indication that the Contracting Parties intended to provide otherwise in their dispute resolution clause, support and confirm an interpretation of Article 13 that allows the host State to raise counterclaims against the claims of the investor.[206]

Where the instrument of consent is framed as a one-way clause, the position is more controversial. Tribunals have considered: **225**

(1) whether such a clause limits the jurisdiction of the Tribunal to considering only claims brought by investors about the obligations of the host State and excludes jurisdiction over counterclaims;[207] or
(2) whether the investor, when electing to submit their claim to arbitration under the ICSID Convention must be taken to have given its consent to the institution of related counterclaims in the same proceeding, thereby conferring jurisdiction on the tribunal to hear such a counterclaim that it might not otherwise have had.[208]

The former construction is more consonant with the terms of such an instrument of consent.[209] It is also consistent with the *travaux* of the ICSID Convention, which suggest that Article 46 was 'in no way intended to extend the jurisdiction of the arbitral tribunal', such that 'in all cases there must be a specific undertaking to admit the question to arbitration'.[210] **226**

In each case, it is necessary to construe the scope of the instrument of consent invoked by the Respondent as the ground upon which it invokes the jurisdiction of the tribunal over its counterclaim. **227**

The second sentence of paragraph (3) adds an important clarification, consistent with the test in the first sentence, which refers only to the instrument of consent *invoked by the respondent*. It serves to emphasise that the claimant may not exclude a counterclaim over which the tribunal would otherwise have jurisdiction by reference to the particular instrument of consent that it invokes or the restrictive manner in which it frames its request: **228**

205 Art 13, Australia–Pakistan BIT (signed 7 February 1998, entered into force 14 October 1998) [1998] ATS 23.
206 *Tethyan*, [1419] (emphasis in the original).
207 *Roussalis* (2011, Hanotiau P, Giardina & Reisman (dissenting on this point)), [869]–[871].
208 Ibid, Declaration, Reisman (dissenting); approved *Goetz*, [279].
209 Atanansova et al 2014: 365–9.
210 ICSID 1969: II, 422 (Broches), 573 (Chairman's Report).

> The investor cannot pick and choose from the dispute resolution provision of a BIT, just like it cannot pick and choose from other provisions of the investment agreement . . . The offer to arbitrate in a BIT's dispute resolution provision can only be accepted according to its own terms. If those terms provide an opportunity for the State to introduce counterclaims, then an investor cannot exclude this possibility by wording its acceptance of the offer narrowly.[211]

229 As Judge Higgins observed in her Separate Opinion in *Oil Platforms*:

> In both civil and common law domestic systems, as in the Rules of the Court, a defendant seeking to bring a counter-claim must show the Court has jurisdiction to pronounce upon them. But it is not essential that the basis of jurisdiction in the claim and in the counterclaim be identical. It is sufficient that there is jurisdiction. (Indeed, were it otherwise, counter-claims in, for example, tort could never be brought, as they routinely are, to actions initiated in contract.)[212]

230 *Paragraph (4)* adds that, in the case of ICSID arbitration, the requirement in Article 42 of the Convention that the counterclaim be 'otherwise within the jurisdiction of the Centre' refers to the outer boundaries set by Article 25 of the ICSID Convention: its requirement that the dispute 'arise directly out of an investment' and that it be 'between a Contracting State . . . and a national of another Contracting State'. It is beyond the scope of this Commentary to elaborate the content of the requisite elements of investment and nationality, as to which there is extensive jurisprudence.[213] The purpose of paragraph (4) is to confirm that these same requirements continue to apply to a tribunal's assessment of a counterclaim.

3 *Admissibility*

231 Where the tribunal does have jurisdiction, it must still additionally consider whether the counterclaim arises directly out of the subject matter of the claim such that it is admissible in the same proceeding. This requirement is also connected to the equality principle. A balanced application of the requirement of sufficient connection ensures that each party's claims arising out of the same dispute can be equally considered together: including such claims whether brought by investor or State, but excluding claims that are extraneous to the dispute.

232 *Paragraph (5)* provides that this requirement is met 'where the counterclaim concerns the same investment that gave rise to the claim'. It adds by way of explanation that this 'does

[211] Lalive and Halonen 2011: 150, [7.30].

[212] *Oil Platforms (Iran v United States of America)* (Order on Counterclaim) [1998] ICJ Rep 190, Separate Opinion of Judge Higgins 217, 218.

[213] McLachlan et al 2017: chs 5 and 6.

not require that the counterclaim be founded upon the same legal instrument or cause of action asserted by the claimant'.

The question of the appropriate test for sufficiency of connection has also arisen in the procedure of other international courts and tribunals. It has been controversial in the practice of the International Court of Justice.[214] The jurisprudence of the Iran–US Claims Tribunal on the matter has been circumscribed by the specific terms of the Algiers Accords, which require that a counterclaim must 'arise out of the same contract, transaction or occurrence'.[215] So the test for the purposes of that Tribunal is the extent of equivalence or symmetry between the counterclaim and the claim: does it arise out of the same contract, transaction or occurrence? For this reason, that Tribunal has not accepted counterclaims between the same parties that are derived from different legal rights and duties, including those arising under generally applicable domestic law. **233**

The subject matter under the ICSID Convention, which falls to be tested to determine whether the requisite connection exists, is the existence of a dispute concerning an investment. This is essentially a matter of factual connection: a question of whether the claim and counterclaim arise out of the same factual matrix. As it was put in the Notes to the ICSID Arbitration Rules (1968): **234**

> [T]o be admissible such claims must arise 'directly' out of the 'subject-matter' of the dispute. The test to satisfy this condition is whether the *factual connection* between the original and the ancillary claim is so close as to require the adjudication of the latter in order to achieve the final settlement of the dispute, the object being to dispose of all the grounds of dispute arising out of the same subject matter.[216]

Paragraph (6) adds two final points of clarification: **235**

(1) It confirms that, where the other requirements of Article 6 are met, the tribunal has power to find a counterclaim admissible 'whether it is founded upon international law or host state law'.
(2) Provided, however, that the counterclaim 'concerns a subject matter that is capable of submission to arbitration'.

Claims founded upon international law. The jurisdiction of the tribunal applies to counterclaims that are founded on legal rights accorded to the respondent State under the terms of the investment treaty. Equally, it may extend to a State's rights against an investor under general international law.[217] **236**

214 Art 80, ICJ Rules of Court was revised in 2000 with effect from 1 February 2001; Antonopoulos 2011.

215 Art II(1), Claims Settlement Declaration 19 January 1981 (1983) 1 Iran–US CTR 9.

216 ICSID Secretariat, Note B(a) to Arbitration Rule 40 of 1968, 1 ICSID Rep 100 (emphasis added); and see *Goetz*, [285].

217 *Urbaser SA v Argentina* (Award) ICSID Case No ARB/07/26 (2016, Bucher P, Martinez-Fraga & McLachlan), [1143], [1187]; *Al-Warraq v Indonesia* (Award) IIC 718 (2014, Cremades P, Hwang & Nariman), [659]–[667].

237 *Claims founded upon host State law.* Tribunals have sometimes expressed the view that a counterclaim under host State law is inadmissible, as it does not invoke 'obligations which share with the primary claim "a common origin, identical sources, and an operational unity"'.[218] This view has subsequently been followed on the basis that public law claims generally fall within the exclusive jurisdiction of the host State courts and cannot be considered as an indivisible part of the claims based on the BIT.[219]

238 This view did not commend itself to the Eighteenth Commission or to the *Institut* as a whole. The Commission took the view that, provided that the Tribunal otherwise has jurisdiction, and the two claims arise factually out of the same investment dispute, there is no reason in principle to exclude *a priori* all claims under the general law of the host State, which is otherwise an applicable source of law for an ICSID Tribunal under Article 42(1) of the Convention.[220]

239 In *Tethyan*, the Tribunal confirmed that 'the scope of consent is not limited to disputes based on Treaty violations but rather extends to disputes based on the investment agreement . . . and/or the regulatory framework for the investment'.[221]

240 This approach would still require a close subject-matter connection between claim and counterclaim. It would not exclude a counterclaim *a priori* on the basis that claims under the domestic law of the host State are of their nature inadmissible.[222] The environmental counterclaims considered in the recent *Ecuador* cases (which were admitted by the consent of both parties) illustrate the capacity of an international arbitral tribunal to consider and rule upon claims founded upon domestic principles of constitutional law that in turn established a regime of liability, compensation and remediation.[223]

241 *Arbitrability.* The final clause of paragraph (6) confirms that this does not enable the State to bring a counterclaim against the investor for a cause of action that is not capable of arbitration. A claim for the enforcement of taxes would, for example, be inadmissible as concerned with the enforcement of sovereign power.[224]

218 *Saluka Investments*, [79]; citing *Klöckner Industrie-Anlagen GmbH v Cameroon* (Award) ICSID Case No ARB/81/2 (1983) 2 ICSID Rep 9.

219 *Paushok v Mongolia* (Award) UNCITRAL (2011, Lalonde P, Grigera Naón & Stern).

220 For a contrary view, see Steingruber 2021.

221 *Tethyan*, [1420].

222 Accord: Douglas 2009: Rule 26.

223 *Perenco Ecuador*; *Burlington Resources* (Decision on Counterclaims).

224 *Computer Sciences Corporation v Iran* (1986) 10 Iran–US CTR 269, 315.

ARTICLE 7:

Third-Person Submissions

(1) Third person submissions may valuably assist a tribunal to determine the dispute, where they bring a perspective, knowledge or insight that is different from that of the disputing parties.

(2) In order to protect the equality of the parties, in accordance with the UNCITRAL Rules on Transparency in Treaty-based Investor–State Arbitration 2014:

- (a) **The third person shall disclose any connection, direct or indirect, which it has with either of the disputing parties, their counsel or members of the tribunal or the subject-matter of the dispute;**
- (b) **The tribunal shall ensure that the disputing parties are given a reasonable opportunity to present their observations on any third person submission; and,**
- (c) **The tribunal shall ensure that any such submission does not unfairly prejudice either disputing party.**

The third context in which the equality principle applies in respect of the parties to a dispute concerns the admission of third-person submissions. This is dealt with in Article 7. 242

The admission of submissions from persons other than the disputing parties, often referred to as *amici curiae*, has been an important procedural innovation in the practice of international investment tribunals in the last decade. 243

Tribunals themselves initiated this practice.[225] States rapidly accepted and codified the practice at the regional level[226] and then internationally: 244

(1) In 2006, the ICSID Administrative Council adopted ICSID Arbitration Rule 37(2), which provides for the Tribunal to allow a non-disputing party to file a written submission.

(2) In 2013, UNCITRAL finalised its Rules on Transparency in Treaty-based Investor–State Arbitration,[227] Article 4 of which provides for submissions by third persons, while Article 5 provides for submissions by States Parties to a Treaty that are not parties to the particular dispute.

225 Alexandrov and Carlson 2010: 49; Boisson de Chazournes 2004; Boisson de Chazournes 2005; *Methanex Corporation v United States of America* (Decision on *Amici Curiae*) 7 ICSID Rep 208 (NAFTA, 2001, Veeder C, Rowley & Christopher); *United Parcel Service of America Inc v Canada* (Decision of the Tribunal on Petitions for Intervention and Participation as *Amici Curiae*) (NAFTA/UNCITRAL, 2001, Keith C, Fortier & Cass); *Aguas Argentinas SA v Argentina* (Order in Response to a Petition for Transparency and Participation as *Amicus Curiae*) ICSID Case No ARB/03/19 (2005, Salacuse P, Kaufmann-Kohler & Nikken).

226 NAFTA FTC 2004.

227 Art 1(2), UNCITRAL Rules on Transparency in Treaty-based Investor–State Arbitration ('UNCITRAL Transparency Rules'), UN Doc A/RES/69/116.

(3) In 2014, the UN General Assembly adopted the United Nations Convention on Transparency in Investor–State Arbitration ('the Mauritius Convention'), which enables States to agree to apply the UNCITRAL Rules to arbitrations under treaties already in force.[228]
(4) In 2018, the ICSID Secretariat proposed a further elaboration of the provisions of the Rules dealing with non-disputing parties.[229] In addition, it proposes a separate rule providing that a non-disputing Treaty Party has the right to file a written submission on the application or interpretation of a treaty at issue in the dispute, with a concomitant right on the part of the parties to make observations on such submission.[230]

245 There have been cognate developments in the practice of some other international tribunals, in particular, under the WTO DSU.[231]

246 The admission in investment arbitration of such submissions has developed in part to meet an equality concern at the constitutional level, where equality is broadly conceived as the maintenance of a balance between public and private interest, so that civil society organisations should be heard before the tribunal where public interests are affected.[232] At the same time, the tribunal must ensure that participation of such third persons does not unfairly prejudice either of the disputing parties in their conduct of the case.

247 The legislative framework that has now been developed for the admission of third-person submissions does not seek to place such persons in the same position as the disputing parties from the point of view of their participation in the procedure. Rather, it recognises that such persons may have a different perspective that nevertheless constitutes a significant interest. So, the UNCITRAL Transparency Rules require the tribunal to evaluate:

(1) whether the third person has a significant interest in the arbitral proceedings; and
(2) the extent to which the submission would assist the arbitral tribunal in the determination of a factual or legal issue related to the arbitral proceedings by bringing a perspective, particular knowledge or insight that is different from that of the disputing parties.[233]

228 United Nations Convention on Transparency in Investor-State Arbitration (adopted by UNGA Res 69/116, 10 December 2014, entry into force 18 October 2017), on which, see Boisson de Chazournes 2015.

229 See now ICSID 2020b: draft Arbitration Rule 67; and see ICSID 2018b.

230 Ibid, Draft Arbitration Rule 68.

231 Boisson de Chazournes and Mbengue 2003; Stern 2005.

232 'An Open Letter about Investor–State Dispute Settlement' (20 April 2015), www.osgoode.yorku.ca/public-statement-international-investment-regime-31-august-2010, [12], maintaining that: 'Private citizens, local communities and civil society organizations should be afforded a right to participate in decision-making that affects their rights and interests, including in the context of investor-state dispute settlement or contract renegotiation. The international investment regime, by not allowing for full and equal participation of such parties alongside the investor where their interests are affected, fails to satisfy this basic requirement of procedural fairness.'

233 Art 4(3)(a) and (b), UNCITRAL Transparency Rules; Rule 37(2), ICSID Arbitration Rules is to like effect.

The UNCITRAL Transparency Rules incorporate a number of features that are designed to ensure that the equality of arms as between the disputing Parties is not prejudiced: **248**

(1) The third person must disclose 'any connection, direct or indirect, which the third person has with any disputing party'.[234]
(2) 'The arbitral tribunal shall ensure that any submission does not disrupt or unduly burden the arbitral proceedings, or unfairly prejudice any disputing party.'[235]
(3) 'The arbitral tribunal shall ensure that the disputing parties are given a reasonable opportunity to present their observations on any submission by the third person.'[236]

Claimants have on occasion expressed concern that the burden of responding to third-person submissions often falls disproportionately on their side.[237] Where satisfied that the third-person submission otherwise meets the criteria, tribunals have tended to address this concern by crafting appropriate procedural directions to limit any undue burden and ensure that both parties have a reasonable opportunity to address the submissions.[238] **249**

234 Art 4(2)(b), ibid.
235 Art 4(5), ibid; to like effect: ICSID Arbitration Rule 37(2).
236 Art 4(6), ibid; to like effect: ICSID Arbitration Rule 37(2).
237 *Bear Creek Mining Corp v Peru* (Procedural Order No 5) ICSID Case No ARB/14/21 (2016, Böckstiegel P, Pryles & Sands), [24].
238 *Biwater Gauff (Tanzania) Ltd v Tanzania* (Procedural Order No 5 *Amicus Curiae*) ICSID Case No ARB/05/22, IIC 32 (2007, Hanotiau P, Born & Landau); *Lilly and Co v Canada* (Procedural Order No 6) UNCT/14/2 (2016, van den Berg P, Bethlehem & Born).

CHAPTER 2: PLEADING AND EVIDENCE

250 Chapter 2 deals with four aspects of pleading and evidence in investment arbitration that have particularly engaged the equality principle:

(1) Article 8 addresses the need to ensure equality of arms in the procedure.
(2) Article 9 concerns the production of documents and evidence.
(3) Article 10 considers objections to production.
(4) Article 11 treats the use of improper means that may disrupt the equality of the parties and imperil the fair conduct of the proceedings.

ARTICLE 8:

Equality of Arms

(1) **The equality of the parties includes the principle of the equality of arms, namely that:**

(a) **Each party shall have the right to be heard on the submissions of the other (*audi alteram partem*); and,**
(b) **Each party shall enjoy reciprocal treatment in the procedural timetable and in matters of pleading, production of documents and evidence.**

(2) **The tribunal should order and enforce a procedural timetable, which promotes both efficiency and equality of the parties.**
(3) **Where, exceptionally, a party is able to establish a compelling case for the admission of late evidence or pleading, the tribunal must be satisfied that, if it admits the evidence or pleading, it is able to afford the other party equality of treatment, including an effective right to be heard on the new material.**
(4) **Equality of treatment in a hearing requires that each party be allocated substantial equality of time to plead and present its evidence; subject always to the tribunal's overall authority to ensure the fair and efficient conduct of the hearing, taking into account the number of witnesses and its own mandate to hear and test the evidence and arguments of the parties.**

1 In General

251 *Paragraph (1).* An important procedural context in which the equality principle is commonly invoked before international investment tribunals is that of ensuring the equality of arms in orders relating to the procedural timetable and the admission into the record of pleadings and evidence. In this context, the equality principle serves two interrelated purposes. It applies to ensure that there is reciprocal treatment of the two parties; it also ensures that each party is given an opportunity to be heard on the

submissions of the other – *audi alteram partem.*[239] This use of the equality principle is applicable to the conduct of proceedings before international courts and tribunals generally.[240]

Paragraph (2). Here, the principle is not in doubt. But its practical application not infrequently gives rise to difficulty as tribunals seek to manage the orderly conduct of the proceedings. There is a distinction to be drawn between the underlying principles of equality of the parties and due process as fundamental rules of procedure and the technical provisions dealing with pleadings and evidence. The tribunal retains discretion to determine how to conduct the proceedings diligently and with procedural economy. The technical rules on pleadings and evidence are not themselves fundamental.[241] **252**

As the ICSID Secretariat notes, its Draft Arbitration Rules 'have been carefully drafted to address efficiency while maintaining the parties' due process rights and equality of treatment. *These are equally important principles.*'[242] **253**

The two principles are not necessarily antipathetic. One party's request for latitude in a previously agreed or ordered timetable may, in fact, result not only in inefficiency, but also in unequal treatment to the other party, which has organised its own pleadings according to the original schedule. This prejudice cannot always be compensated by corresponding adjustments for the other party. The enforcement of a previously agreed or ordered procedural timetable may itself be an important vindication of the equality principle, depending on the circumstances. As a result the tribunal must decide whether the first party's request is actually necessary to afford that party due process *and* the effect on the equality of treatment of the other party. These considerations are borne out in a review of the pertinent tribunal practice. **254**

Paragraph (3). The equality of arms has a particular application to the admission of evidence. A tribunal may decide to exclude evidence if it finds that this basic condition has not been, or cannot be, met: **255**

> Generally, international tribunals take a liberal approach to the admissibility of evidence. The Tribunal is of the view, however, that such discretion is not absolute. In the Tribunal's judgment, there are limits to its discretion derived from principles of general application in international arbitration, whether pursuant to the Washington Convention or under other forms of international arbitration. Good faith and procedural fairness being among such principles, the Tribunal should refuse to admit evidence into the proceedings if,

239 See generally, della Cananea 2016: ch 3.

240 Cheng 1953: 295.

241 *Venezuela v Tenaris SA* (Decision on Annulment, ICSID Case No ARB/12/23 (2018, Knieper P, Moreno Rodríguez & Piérola Castro), [91].

242 ICSID 2018c: [33] (emphasis added). For the difficulties of maintaining efficiency while at the same time respecting due process that can be encountered in practice, see: Berger and Jensen 2016; Reed 2017.

depending on the circumstances under which it was obtained and tendered to the other Party and the Tribunal, there are good reasons to believe that those principles of good faith and procedural fairness have not been respected. The foregoing finds confirmation in the IBA Rules on the Taking of Evidence, to which reference may be made as guidelines. Article 9(1) states: 'The Arbitral Tribunal shall determine the admissibility, relevance, materiality and weight of evidence.' Article 9(2)(g) of the Rules provides that evidence may be excluded in the presence of '*considerations of fairness or equality of the Parties that the Arbitral Tribunal determines to be compelling.*'[243]

256 Evidence has been declared inadmissible where a claimant initially withheld evidence and then sought to admit it on the eve of the hearing.[244] So too where a respondent sought to adduce testimony of expert witnesses given in a prior proceeding to which the respondent, but not the claimant, had been party. In this instance, the Tribunal considered that the material should be excluded since there was an unavoidable risk of use of the prior testimony out of its original context 'against which Claimants would have no equal means of defence'.[245] A tribunal may also decide to order the production of material from an earlier case to which only one party was privy, in order to ensure an equal knowledge of all elements of the case before it.

257 *Paragraph (4).* In principle, time is allocated equally between the parties at the hearing. However, exceptions are justified where the number of witnesses and experts called by one party substantially exceeds the number of witnesses and experts called by the other, as a strict application of the principle of equal division of time may impair a party's opportunity to cross-examine the witnesses and experts it designated. The principle of equal division of time has to be applied with a certain flexibility to take into account an unequal number of witnesses and experts and the overall fair and efficient conduct of the proceedings.[246]

258 Two issues require particular mention in the application of Article 8(3):

(1) the late submission of new evidence or arguments after the close of written pleadings; and
(2) the submission of evidence after the hearing.

243 *EDF (Services) Ltd v Romania* (Procedural Order No 3) ICSID Case No ARB/05/13, IIC 394 (2008, Bernardini P, Derains & Rovine), [47] (emphasis in the original).

244 Ibid, [48].

245 *Beccara v Argentina* (Procedural Order No 3) ICSID Case No ARB/07/5, IIC 418 (2010, Tercier P, Abi-Saab & van den Berg), [147]; see also *Abaclat v Argentina* (Procedural Order No 11) ICSID Case No ARB/07/5, IIC 809 (2012, van den Berg P, Tercier & Torres Bernárdez), [33]–[34].

246 *Abaclat v Argentina* (Procedural Order No 28) ICSID Case No ARB/07/5 (2014, Tercier P, van den Berg & Torres Bernárdez (dissenting)), 6; *Gabriel Resources Ltd v Romania* (Procedural Order No 25) ICSID Case No ARB/15/31 (2019, Tercier P, Grigera Naón & Douglas), [17]–[19]; Ulmer 2010: 243–4: 'in certain cases, a chess-clock system can inhibit fair and proper administration of the case in favour of a rigid false "equality" between the parties'.

2 *Late Submissions*

When new evidence or arguments are introduced late in proceedings, the tribunal must balance equally the rights of both the party that seeks to introduce the new material and the right of the other party to have a fair opportunity to contest it.[247] Depending upon the circumstances, application of the equality principle can result in the exclusion of late and unauthorised submissions or evidence if the tribunal is otherwise unable to afford the other party an adequate opportunity for contradiction.[248] As one Annulment Committee recently observed: 'An ICSID tribunal's task is to provide a party with a reasonable opportunity to be heard; there is no right to an unlimited opportunity to be heard. It is for the party concerned to take advantage of that opportunity, when provided.'[249] **259**

As the Iran–US Claims Tribunal put it: **260**

> Article 15 of the Tribunal Rules requires that the Tribunal treat the parties equally. This is a fundamental principle of justice. In the circumstances of these cases, the delicate balance of equality would be tipped if one party were to be permitted to present an extensive Memorial and additional exhibits, without providing an opportunity for the other party to file a memorial in response. While the filing by Claimants of their Memorial on the Merits prior to the Hearing may be an advantage to the Respondents in that it informs them in detail of Claimants' contentions and arguments and may be of assistance to the Tribunal in analyzing the case, nevertheless it cannot be accepted without

247 See *Grand River Enterprises Six Nations Ltd v United States of America* (Decision on Jurisdiction) 15 ICSID Rep 503, IIC 128 (NAFTA, 2006, Nariman P, Anaya & Crook), [95]–[102]; *Niko Resources (Bangladesh) Ltd v Bangladesh Petroleum Exploration & Production Co Ltd ('Bapex')* (Procedural Order No 11) ICSID Case No ARB/10/11 and ARB/10/18 (2015, Schneider P, McLachlan & Paulsson); *South American Silver Ltd v Bolivia* (Procedural Order No 22) PCA 2013–15 (2016, Zuleta Jaramillo P, César Guglielmino & Orrego Vicuña), [32]–[33]; *Von Pezold v Zimbabwe* (Procedural Order No 7) ICSID Case Nos ARB/10/15 and ARB/10/25 (2014, Fortier P, Hwang & Williams), [57]; *Nelson v Mexico* (Procedural Order No 11) ICSID Case No UNCT/17/1 (2018, Zuleta P, Veeder & Mariano Gomezperalta), [18]–[20].

248 *Application of the Convention on the Prevention and Punishment of the Crime of Genocide (Bosnia and Herzegovina v Serbia and Montenegro)* (Judgment) [2007] ICJ Rep 43, [54]. See also *Avena (Mexico v United States of America)* (Judgment) [2004] ICJ Rep 12, [7]–[8]; *Indus Waters Kishenganga Arbitration (Pakistan v India)* (Partial Award) PCA Case No 2011–01 (2013) 154 ILR 1, [113]–[117]; *Craig v Ministry of Energy of Iran* (Award) (1983) 3 Iran–US CTR 280; *Dames and Moore v Iran* (Award) (1983) 4 Iran–US CTR 212; *Morrison-Knudsen Pacific Ltd v Iran* (1986) 7 Iran–US CTR 70; *MEMCCO v Iran* (Award) (1986) 9 Iran–US CTR 340; *Futura Trading Inc v National Iranian Oil Co* (Award) (1986) 13 Iran–US CTR 99, 101.

249 *Zimbabwe v von Pezold* (Decision on Annulment) ICSID Case No ARB/10/15 (2018, Heiskanen P, Kalicki & Kettani), [255], concluding that there was no denial of the right to be heard and therefore no breach of a fundamental rule of procedure. See also proposed Arbitration Rule 3(2), which sets out a general duty on the Tribunal to treat the parties equally and provide each party with a reasonable opportunity to present its case: ICSID 2020b: 33.

> providing the Respondents an equal opportunity to make a written submission.[250]

261 More commonly, the tribunal will only admit the new material on condition that it can adjust the timetable so as to give the other party an adequate right to be heard on it, whether by submitting a further pleading or piece of evidence.

262 The Iran–US Claims Tribunal has summarised the applicable principles in terms of more general application:

> First, Articles 22 and 23 of the Rules provide authority for the Tribunal to establish deadlines for the submission of written submissions. In establishing such deadlines, however, the Tribunal must be mindful of Article 15, which requires that both Parties be treated with equality. . . . Taken together, these rules provide authority for the Tribunal to make and to enforce deadlines for the filing of written submissions, provided that the Parties are treated with equality. This limitation is important. Equality, a 'fundamental principle of justice', implies that the Parties must have equal opportunity to make written submissions and to respond to each other's submissions. . . . In determining whether to admit a late submission, the Tribunal has frequently referred to these fundamental requirements of equality between, and fairness to, the Parties, and the possible prejudice to either Party. Further, the orderly conduct of the proceedings also requires that time limits be established and enforced. In applying these principles to the specific facts of a case, however, the Tribunal considers the character and contents of late-filed documents and the length and cause of the delay. These factors affect the probability of prejudice, the equality of treatment of the Parties, and the disruption of the arbitral process by the delay.[251]

3 Submission of New Evidence after the Hearing

263 Particular problems in ensuring the equality of the parties may arise where one party seeks to adduce new evidence after the hearing. In this situation, affording the other party a proper opportunity to exercise its right of contradiction may pose particular difficulties. The witnesses will already have given their evidence and been tested on it. The new material may not be capable of being tested in the same way. It may affect the way in which the other party wishes to plead its case. The Tribunal has a power to reopen a proceeding 'on the ground that new evidence is forthcoming, or that there is a vital need for clarification on certain specific points',[252] but this must always be exceptional. It may simply ask for additional evidence on a particular

[250] *Foremost Tehran Inc v Iran* (Order) (1983) 3 Iran–US CTR 361; and see *Iran v United States of America (Case Nos A3, A8, A9, A14 and B61)* (Order) (2005) 38 Iran–US CTR 153, [9]–[10].

[251] *Harris Int'l Telecommunications Inc v Iran* (Award) (1987) 17 Iran–US CTR 31, [58]–[62].

[252] ICSID Arbitration Rule 38(2).

point, provided it gives the parties the opportunity to comment in writing on the new material.[253]

If a tribunal does decide exceptionally to admit new evidence after the hearing, particular attention in this regard must be paid to the equality principle. An Annulment Committee has observed that:[254] **264**

> The right to present one's case, or 'principe de la contradiction,'[255] in arbitral proceedings includes the right of each party to make submissions on evidence presented by its opponent.[256] If an arbitral tribunal fails to accord such a right, then its award will be subject to annulment.[257] One example of this principle being applied in the international commercial arbitration context is where the arbitral tribunal has permitted one of the parties to adduce additional documentary evidence after the oral hearing, without giving the other party the opportunity to comment on it.[258]

The same approach has been applied in other international courts and tribunals.[259] It has also been upheld under international human rights instruments.[260] **265**

253 *Venezuela v Tenaris*, [249].

254 *Fraport AG Frankfurt Airport Services Worldwide v The Philippines* (Decision on Annulment) ICSID Case No ARB/03/25 (2010, Tomka P, Hascher & McLachlan), [200], internal citations included.

255 Gaillard and Savage 1999: 947–8, [1638]; Poudret and Besson 2007: [546]–[554].

256 Born 2009: 2582–3.

257 Ibid, and the numerous authorities there cited.

258 See, e.g., *Rice Trading (Guyana) Ltd v Nidera Handelscompagnie BV* (Hague Court of Appeal) (28 April 1998) (1998) XXIII YB Comm Arb 731.

259 Cheng 1953: 295; *Legal Status of Eastern Greenland (Denmark v Norway)* (1933) PCIJ Rep, Ser A/B No 53, 25–6; *Chorzów Factory (Germany v Poland)* (1928) PCIJ Rep, Ser A No 17, 7, where the Permanent Court afforded a party a further opportunity to be heard on new evidence or submissions submitted by its opposing party. Specific recognition of this principle in relation to submissions made, or evidence produced, after the closure of written and oral proceedings, is given in Arts 56 and 72, ICJ Rules of Court.

260 *Feldbrugge* (29 May 1986) ECHR Ser A, No 99, 8 EHRR 425, [44].

ARTICLE 9:

Production of Documents and Evidence

(1) **During the written phase, each party shall produce to the other the evidence on which it relies, so that the other party has a reasonable opportunity to respond.**
(2) **The same standards shall be applied to adjudge the requests of both parties for the production of specific documents. The IBA Rules on the Taking of Evidence in International Arbitration 2010 provide a useful general framework for such determinations.**
(3) **In ordering a timetable for production, the tribunal should take into account the particular challenges faced by States, especially developing States, in locating and producing documents. This must be balanced against ensuring that the other party has an adequate opportunity to consider and respond to the documents within the procedural timetable.**
(4) **Where the investor is part of a group of companies, the principles of equality and good faith require that it should use best efforts to produce relevant documents that are held by its parent or affiliated companies or shareholders, when the respondent State so requests and the tribunal so directs.**
(5) **Where a party has requested the attendance of a witness for cross-examination at the hearing and the party relying on the evidence of that witness fails without a valid reason to produce that witness, the tribunal may (save in exceptional circumstances) disregard that evidence in order to preserve the procedural equilibrium between the parties.**

266 One procedural context in which international investment tribunals have frequently had to apply considerations of the equality of the parties is in their treatment of evidentiary issues. A highly practical application of the principle, its satisfactory application in this context also has wider implications. As Kazazi has observed:

> The intervention of international tribunals in matters of evidence is to take place impartially and with due regard to the fundamental principles of equality of parties and the necessity of providing parties with a full opportunity to present their claims and defences. The misapplication of this delicate task, which is usually fulfilled satisfactorily by knowledgeable and experienced judges and arbitrators, is not only prejudicial to the rights of parties in a particular case but harmful to the regime of international judicial and arbitral settlement of disputes as a whole.[261]

267 Investment tribunals are endowed with a broad discretion on questions of evidence. ICSID Arbitration Rule 34(1) provides that: 'The Tribunal shall be the judge of the admissibility of any evidence adduced and of its probative value.' The consequence is that:

[261] Kazazi 1995: 155.

As a tribunal enjoys discretion on matters of evidence and the burden of proof, its assessment can only constitute a deviation from a fundamental rule of procedure if it violates the integrity of the procedure and the basic requirement of equal treatment and the right to be heard.[262]

Parties and Tribunals in investment disputes now commonly agree to refer to the IBA Rules on the Taking of Evidence in International Arbitration 2010 ('IBA Rules 2010') as guidance. These Rules also confirm that: 'The Arbitral Tribunal shall determine the admissibility, relevance, materiality and weight of evidence.'[263] At the same time, they reflect underlying considerations of equality, confirming as general principles 'that each Party shall act in good faith and be entitled to know, reasonably in advance of any Evidentiary Hearing or any fact or merits determination, the evidence on which the other Parties rely'.[264] The Rules expressly enjoin tribunals to consider the equality of the Parties in making any determination to exclude evidence.[265] **268**

Tribunals have had to consider the practical application of the equality principle at each stage in the evidentiary process: **269**

(1) the production of documentary evidence;
(2) its admissibility;
(3) the exclusion of evidence on grounds of privilege, including State secrecy;
(4) the cross-examination of witnesses at the hearing; and
(5) the evaluation of evidence that has been adduced.

The general treatment of evidence in order to ensure the equality of arms is dealt with in Article 8. The exclusion of evidence on grounds of State secrecy gives rise to problems that, while not unique to investment disputes, frequently arise in this context, since such disputes are of their nature concerned with challenges to the international legality of the decisions of organs of the State. The particular issues in the application of the equality principle to which this gives rise will be examined in the commentary on Article 10. The admissibility of evidence that has been unlawfully obtained or through the use of a State's powers of criminal investigation also requires separate treatment under Article 11. **270**

Article 9 deals in particular with (1) document production (paragraphs (1)—(4)) and (2) attendance of witnesses (paragraph (5)). **271**

262 *Micula v Romania* (Decision on Annulment) ICSID Case No ARB/05/20, IIC 772 (2016, von Wobeser P, Cremades & Yusuf), [265].
263 Art 9(1).
264 Preamble (3).
265 Arts 9(2)(g) and 9(3)(e).

1 Document Production

272 A party is generally obliged to produce to its opponent documents on which it relies since 'it is contrary to the principle of the equality of arms that one party has access to and can rely on documents to which the other party has no access'.[266]

273 Inequality does not arise simply from the fact that a request for production by one party is allowed while a request by another party is denied, or from the fact that one party has to produce a large number of documents and the other none or very few. Each request by each party must be considered and determined by the tribunal on its own individual merits. It is only where it can be shown that a tribunal has applied inconsistent standards in the way in which it has treated the requests of the different parties that there can be said to be inequality of treatment.[267]

274 Application of the equality principle to the production phase does not preclude tribunals from showing some flexibility as to the timing of production in recognition of the administrative challenges faced by States – in particular, in developing countries – in locating and producing relevant documents from across its civil service.[268] This must be balanced with ensuring that the claimant has an adequate opportunity within the timetable to respond to the documents so produced.

275 The arbitral process itself places limits on how far a tribunal can go to assure equality of information, particularly in cases in which one party, whether claimant or respondent, is a repeat litigant and has wider experience arising from other cases. As one tribunal observed in relation to the case before it:

> Evidently the Respondent and its legal advisers have a synoptic view of the various disputes related to the oil industry in Ecuador which may be denied to the Claimant and its legal advisers. But that is a natural inequality as between private companies and a host State, one which arises from their respective status and roles and which cannot be reversed *en tant que tel*.[269]

276 At the same time, the tribunal must be astute to consider equality in the production of evidence in substance and not simply in form:

266 *Standard Chartered Bank (Hong Kong) Ltd v Tanzania Electric Supply Co Ltd* (Procedural Order No 6) ICSID Case No ARB/10/20 (2012, McRae P, Douglas & Stern), [13].

267 *Azurix Corporation v Argentina* (Decision on Annulment) ICSID Case No ARB/01/02, IIC 388 (2009, Griffith P, Ajibola & Hwang), [233]; *Pey Casado and Président Allende Foundation v Chile* (Decision on Annulment) ICSID Case No ARB/98/2, IIC 569 (2012, Fortier P, Bernardini & El-Kosheri), [325].

268 *Amco Asia Corporation v Indonesia* (Decision on Annulment) ICSID Case No ARB/81/1, (1986) 1 ICSID Rep 509 (Seidl-Hohenveldern P, Feliciano & Giardina), [90]; *SARL Benvenuti & Bonfant v Congo* (Award) (1980) 1 ICSID Rep 335 (Trolle P, Bystricky & Razafindralambo), [1.29], [1.33]; *Railroad Development Corporation v Guatemala* (Decision on Provisional Measures) ICSID Case No ARB/07/23, IIC 352 (2008, Rigo Sureda P, Crawford & Eizenstat), [15], [33]; Wälde 2010: 161, 181.

269 *EnCana Corporation v Ecuador* (Partial Award on Jurisdiction) LCIA Case No UN3481, UNCITRAL (2004) 12 ICSID Rep 413 (Crawford P, Barrera Sweeney & Grigera Naón), [43].

(1) The State Party is answerable before an international tribunal in respect of 'any State organ . . . whatever position it holds in the organization of the State, and whatever its character as an organ . . . of the State'.[270] In its practical application to production of documents, this can require a very wide search, which may place particular burdens on States, especially developing States.

(2) In the case of an investor, while respecting separate corporate personality, a tribunal must also strive to ensure that this does not operate to limit searches for probative evidence where, in fact, the party appearing before it has the practical ability to seek and obtain relevant documents from its parent or sister companies within the same group or with the same ultimate beneficial owner. '[G]ood faith also imposes a duty of best efforts to obtain documents that are in the possession of entities or persons with whom or with which the party the subject of the request has a relevant relationship.'[271] This can, in some circumstances, apply to a claimant company's shareholders.

These considerations led the Commission to prepare paragraphs (3) and (4). **277**

2 *Attendance of Witnesses*

The ICSID Arbitration Rules provide for the examination of witnesses before the tribunal,[272] but also permit the tribunal to admit evidence by way of written deposition only.[273] **278**

The IBA Rules nevertheless provide that if a witness whose appearance has been requested by a party fails without a valid reason to appear for testimony at the hearing, 'the Arbitral Tribunal *shall* disregard any Witness Statement related to that Evidentiary Hearing by that witness, unless, in exceptional circumstances, the Arbitral Tribunal decides otherwise'.[274] **279**

An important rationale for this rule is to preserve the equality of the parties. Where a party does not produce its witnesses and experts designated or ordered to appear for cross-examination at the hearing, the tribunal cannot rely on their statements 'without breaching the procedural equilibrium that should exist between the parties'.[275] **280**

For the same reason, a party's withdrawal of its designation of a witness for cross-examination may also provoke inequality where it 'would lead to a prejudicial imbalance and would prevent a comparative assessment of the credibility of the key witnesses'. Thus, **281**

270 Art 4(2), International Law Commission, Articles on the Responsibility of States for Internationally Wrongful Acts 2001.

271 *Gallo v Canada* (Procedural Order No 2) PCA Case No 2008–02 (NAFTA, 2009, Fernández-Armesto P, Castel & Thomas), [8].

272 Rule 35(1).

273 Rule 36(a).

274 Art 4(7), IBA Rules 2010 (emphasis added).

275 *Metalpar SA and Buen Aire SA v Argentina* (Award) ICSID Case No ARB/03/5, IIC 326 (2008, Oreamuno P, Cameron & Chabaneix), [153]–[155].

a tribunal may reject a party's request to withdraw witnesses from cross-examination 'in order to ensure that the Arbitral Tribunal will receive a balanced picture on key issues and to guarantee equal treatment of the Parties'.[276]

282 The Tribunal has the power to call upon the parties to produce witnesses and experts.[277] One reason for the exercise of that power may be for the purpose of 'ensuring equality of arms and holding the ring between the parties',[278] by providing for the availability of a witness whose testimony is within the power of one party and which the other party considers relevant to the issues in the case.

283 The Commission took the view that the failure to produce a witness called for cross-examination may engage the equality principle, but that the formulation in the IBA Rules was too inflexible. Paragraph (5) is therefore phrased permissively, confirming the power of the tribunal.[279]

284 *Evaluation*. The position at the stage when, having heard the parties, the tribunal turns to its own evaluation of the evidence is quite different. Since the evaluation of evidence is within the discretion of the tribunal, 'an applicant's dissatisfaction with the way a tribunal has exercised its discretion in evaluating evidence cannot be a basis for a finding that there has been unequal treatment and hence a violation of a fundamental rule of procedure necessitating annulment'.[280]

[276] *Abaclat v Argentina* (Procedural Order No 28) ICSID Case No ARB/07/5 (2014, van den Berg P, Tercier & Torres Bernárdez (dissenting)), 4.

[277] Rule 34(2)(a).

[278] *Tulip Real Estate Investment and Development Netherlands BV v Turkey* (Decision on Annulment) ICSID Case No ARB/11/28, IIC 756 (2015) (Tomka P, Booth & Schreuer), [147].

[279] (2019) 79 *Annuaire* 614 (Kazazi), 616 (McLachlan).

[280] *Tulip*, [84]–[85].

ARTICLE 10:

Objections to Production

(1) The tribunal shall apply the equality principle in making decisions with regard to pleas of privilege from disclosure, in light of the fact that the applicable standards may differ between the national laws of the parties. The tribunal should strive to apply a standard that operates equally for both parties.

(2) Where the parties raise objections to disclosure with regard to documents on grounds of, respectively, commercial confidentiality or State secrecy, the tribunal should strive to secure a balance of treatment between the parties so as to ensure that each party has the ability to obtain evidence that is relevant and material to the issues in dispute, whilst at the same time respecting the wider interests of each party beyond the instant case and relevant policy considerations.

(3) In the case of a plea of State secrecy, the tribunal shall balance the public interest in the administration of justice which supports disclosure against the public interest underlying the confidentiality of governmental communications.

(4) In so doing, it should invite the parties to agree protocols for the protection of confidentiality or secrecy in documents or parts thereof applicable in the case before the tribunal.

(5) In a case in which an objection to production is raised:

- **(a) The objection must be justified with sufficient specificity in order to enable the opposing party to contest it and the objection to be determined;**
- **(b) The tribunal has discretion whether to accept the objection, balancing the public interests involved;**
- **(c) The tribunal shall apply international law to its decision on the objection;**
- **(d) The tribunal should, in appropriate cases, consider, in consultation with the parties, appointing an independent third party expert to review the documents and decide contested objections to production.**

The commentary below deals in particular with (1) legal professional privilege, (2) State secret privilege and (3) process. **285**

For this reason, the IBA Rules 2010 expressly enjoin tribunals to consider the equality of the parties in making any determination to exclude evidence.[281] The commentary to those rules suggests that the need to protect fairness and equality particularly arises where different approaches to privilege from disclosure may apply in the home jurisdictions of the respective disputing parties. It indicates that the tribunal may be justified in excluding documents that may be privileged from production in one country, but not in the other.[282] **286**

Investment tribunals have taken the same approach, deciding that in order to avoid 'a clear imbalance in the treatment of the parties in the proceedings . . . the Parties should be bound **287**

[281] Arts 9(2)(g) and 9(3)(e).

[282] IBA Commentary 2010: 25–6.

by the standard that affords the broadest protection and that protects the expectations of both parties in international arbitration'.[283]

288 Article 10 makes general provision for objections to production in paragraphs (1) and (2), followed by a specific test in case of an objection on grounds of State secrecy (3). The remainder of Article 10 is devoted to the procedure for resolving objections to production, either by agreement (4) or order (5).

289 The exclusion of evidence from production on grounds of privilege from disclosure may have particular implications for the equality of the parties.[284] Upholding a claim to privilege prevents a party from having access to otherwise relevant material that may enable it to prosecute its claim or defence. At the same time, where a ground of privilege from disclosure is found to apply, the tribunal must take care to apply it in an equal manner as between the parties.

1 Legal Professional Privilege

290 A plea of legal professional privilege is equally available to States as to private parties. Its application is a matter of law, not discretion.[285] It rests on the same interest in protecting the confidential communication of legal advice, whether given by external or internal counsel. In the government context, the privilege is not defeated by circulation beyond the attorney and the particular official requesting or providing the information, provided such confidentiality is maintained.[286]

2 State Secret Privilege

291 Different considerations apply where the grounds alleged for exclusion are State secrecy. This category is accepted in the IBA Rules 2010 as:

> [G]rounds of special political or institutional sensitivity (including evidence that has been classified as secret by a government or a public international institution) that the Arbitral Tribunal determines to be compelling.[287]

This ground was introduced with equality considerations in mind, in order 'to put such special political or institutional sensitivity on an equal footing with commercial or technical confidentiality'.[288]

283 *Poštová banka, as v Greece* (Procedural Order No 6) ICSID Case No ARB/13/8 (2014, Zuleta P, Stern & Townsend), [14]–[16].

284 See generally Sheppard 2016.

285 Art 9(2)(b), IBA Rules 2010; *Niko Resources Bangladesh Ltd v Bangladesh Petroleum Exploration & Production Co Ltd* (Procedural Order No 22) ICSID Case Nos ARB/10/11 and 10/18 (2017, Schneider P, McLachlan & Paulsson), [22].

286 *Glamis Gold Ltd v United States of America* (Decision on Document Production – Privilege) IIC 126 (NAFTA, 2005, Young P, Caron & Hubbard), [21]–[24].

287 Art 9(2)(f).

288 IBA Commentary 2010: 26.

In investment cases, it is likely to have a particular application. Such cases of their nature concern the international legality of a State measure. Some internal documents produced in the course of the decision to impose such a measure may be privileged from disclosure under the internal law of the State. Yet, documents relating to such a process may be highly germane to the claimant's claim. If a State were permitted to deploy its own national law to avoid its obligation to produce all such documents, this would create an imbalance between the parties. A 'self-judging blanket exclusion' would be unacceptable as 'one of the most fundamental principles of international arbitration that the parties should be treated with equality'.[289] Claims of this kind must therefore be determined by reference to general principles of law commonly applied by international tribunals, rather than the national law of the State concerned.[290] This consideration is reflected in paragraph (5)(c), which requires the tribunal to apply international law to its decision on the objection. **292**

The imbalance cannot be resolved by simply extending the privilege to the claimant, as it will not necessarily be relevant to the claimant's evidence and may not be matched by commercial confidentiality considerations on the part of the claimant. An overly broad application of State secrecy as a basis for excluding evidence from production could therefore undermine the fundamental objective of equality between the parties that motivated the establishment of international tribunals as an independent forum for the resolution of investment disputes. **293**

In light of these considerations, this ground for exclusion – in contrast to legal professional privilege – is not absolute. The tribunal 'must take into account Claimant's interest in the production of said documents in order to determine whether [Respondent's] interests in withholding the documents are outweighed'.[291] The tribunal must also find the grounds for exclusion to be 'compelling'.[292] **294**

These factors are reflected in paragraph (3), which requires the tribunal to balance the public interest in the administration of justice, which supports disclosure, against the public interest underlying the confidentiality of governmental communication. **295**

289 *Biwater Gauff (Tanzania) Ltd v Tanzania* (Procedural Order No 2) ICSID Case No ARB/05/22, IIC 82 (2006, Hanotiau P, Born & Landau), 8–9; see also Wälde 2010: 161, 174.

290 *Churchill Mining Plc and Planet Mining Pty Ltd v Indonesia* (Decision on Annulment) ICSID Case Nos ARB/12/14 and ARB/12/40 (2019, Hascher P; Böckstiegel & Kalicki), [211]. However, the degree of political or institutional sensitivity may be measured to a certain extent by reference to domestic law: *Global Telecom Holding SAE v Canada* (Procedural Order No 4) ICSID Case No ARB/16/16 (2018, Affaki P, Born & Lowe), [39].

291 *Gallo v Canada* (Procedural Order No 3) (NAFTA, 2009, Fernández-Armesto P, Castel & Thomas), [53].

292 Art 9(2)(f), IBA Rules 2010.

3 Process

296 The respondent State that invokes State secrecy as a ground for the exclusion of documents must go beyond assertion and provide sufficient information to the tribunal in order to enable it to identify the documents with particularity and to understand the nature of the secrecy interest alleged.[293] As one tribunal put it: 'The principle of equality in the treatment of the parties laid down by Article 15 of the UNCITRAL Arbitration Rules governing these proceedings also requires that such privileges be clearly explained so as to allow the Investor the opportunity to provide informed comments on the matter.'[294] The same approach applies in the case of the assertion by a claimant of commercial or technical confidentiality.[295]

297 The responsible official asserting such a privilege on behalf of the State should first assess whether the documents in question fall within a category that may justify the claim of privilege and then weigh whether the public interest in withholding disclosure outweighs the public interest in the fair administration of justice that is promoted by disclosure.[296]

298 Where the ground of privilege relates to the government's deliberative process itself, especially at Executive or Cabinet level, tribunals have generally required that the material is sufficiently segregated and identified so that the tribunal is in a position to evaluate the assertions of the officials who request the privilege.[297]

299 In some circumstances, tribunals have appointed an independent person to review documents over which a claim to privilege from production is asserted and to report to the tribunal.[298] This is provided for in paragraph (5)(d).

300 Documents that have been exchanged between the States Parties to the Treaty (but are not in the public domain) fall into a category that particularly require production. They may be relevant to the interpretation of the relevant objections under the provisions of Articles 31 and 32 of the Vienna Convention on the Law of Treaties and both disputing parties should be equally entitled to advance submissions on the basis of the same record. As one NAFTA Tribunal observed:

293 *Pope and Talbot Inc v Canada* (Ruling on Claim of Crown Privilege) (2000) 7 ICSID Rep 99, [1.4]–[1.5]; see also *SD Myers Inc v Canada* (Explanatory Note to Procedural Order No 10) (1999) 8 ICSID Rep 13 (Hunter P, Chiasson & Schwartz), [5], following WTO, *Canada – Measures affecting the export of civilian aircraft* (Panel Report) (14 April 1999) WT/DS70/R.

294 *Merrill & Ring Forestry LP v Canada* (Decision on Document Production) (NAFTA, 2008, Orrego Vicuña P, Dam & Rowley), [18]–[21]; see also *Tennant Energy LLC v Canada* (Procedural Order No 1) PCA Case No 2018–54 (2019, Bull P, Doak Bishop & Bethlehem), [7.4].

295 *South American Silver Ltd v Bolivia* (Procedural Order No 7 – Document Production) PCA Case No 2013–15 (2015, Zuleta Jaramillo P, Guglielmino & Orrego Vicuña), [21].

296 *United Parcel Service of America Inc v Canada* (Decision on Canada's Claim of Cabinet Privilege) IIC 267 (NAFTA, 2004, Keith P, Cass & Fortier), [9], citing common law authorities on public interest immunity (for a current statement of which, see now *Al-Rawi v Security Service* [2011] UKSC 34, [2012] 1 AC 531, [145] per Lord Clarke (dissenting but not on this point)).

297 *Glamis Gold*, [36]; *Merrill & Ring Forestry*, [19].

298 *Foresti v South* Africa (Award) ICSID Case No ARB(AF)/07/1 (2010, Lowe P, Brower & Matthews), [14]; *Guyana v Suriname* (Procedural Order No 1) PCA Case No 2004–04 (UNCLOS, 2005), [4]–[5].

> [H]ad the dispute arisen between any of the NAFTA Parties rather than between one of the NAFTA Parties and a private party, the parties to the arbitration would have had equal access to the negotiating history of the Agreement as well as equal opportunity to resort to those documents. In this context, the Tribunal finds it consistent with the principle of equality that the parties to this arbitration are given the same opportunity to present their case, including the opportunity for the private party to access existing documents of the types specified above which are freely available to the government party, irrespective of whether such documents are ultimately conclusive as to any issue in dispute.[299]

[299] *Canfor Corporation v United States of America* (Procedural Order No 5) (NAFTA, 2004, Gaillard P, Harper & Weiler), [22].

ARTICLE 11:

Improper Means

(1) **Both parties owe a duty to each other and to the tribunal to conduct themselves in the proceedings in good faith.**
(2) **The tribunal has the power to exclude evidence where it is satisfied that it has been obtained in violation of the principle of good faith and that it is essential to do so in order to preserve the equality of the parties.**
(3) **Exceptionally, in order to protect the fairness of its own procedure and the equality of the parties, the tribunal may recommend to the State measures concerning the effect of the exercise of its powers of criminal investigation and prosecution upon the tribunal's own process.**
(4) **In such a case, the tribunal will only act on the basis of clear evidence of conduct that is aimed at obtaining an unfair advantage in the proceedings before it or otherwise imperils the fair conduct of those proceedings.**

1 Context

301 A further context in which investment arbitral tribunals have invoked the principle of the equality of the parties has been in the deployment by a party of bad faith tactics in the collection or suppression of evidence.[300]

302 This principle applies equally to both parties. In *Methanex Corp v United States of America*, the Tribunal held, excluding evidence unlawfully obtained by the Claimant:

> [T]he Disputing Parties each owed in this arbitration a general legal duty to the other and to the Tribunal to conduct themselves in good faith during these arbitral proceedings and to respect the equality of arms between them, the principles of 'equal treatment' and procedural fairness being also required by Article 15(1) of the UNCITRAL Rules. As a general principle, therefore, just as it would be wrong for the USA *ex hypothesi* to misuse its intelligence assets to spy on Methanex (and its witnesses) and to introduce into evidence the resulting materials into this arbitration, so too would it be wrong for Methanex to introduce evidential materials obtained by Methanex unlawfully.[301]

303 Nevertheless, the State has at its disposal a range of criminal law powers that are not available to private litigants. Abuse of such powers in order to seek to affect the balance of the evidence in an investment arbitration would breach the equality principle and also the duty to arbitrate in good faith.

[300] See Blair and Gojković 2018.
[301] *Methanex Corporation v United States of America* (Award) 44 ILM 1345 (NAFTA, 2005, Veeder P, Reisman & Rowley), Part II Ch 1, [54].

Particular issues that have arisen in this context are the intimidation of witnesses and party representatives in order to discourage them from giving evidence or assisting in the claim, including through the pursuit of criminal proceedings;[302] and the use of criminal enforcement powers to obtain evidence by illegitimate means, such that the particular coercive act is not being employed for its proper purpose. For example, a police investigation may be used not to detect crime, but rather as a means of obtaining discovery for use in the arbitration. At the same time, tribunals must give appropriate deference to the sovereign prerogative to investigate and prosecute crime in the public interest. **304**

The reported jurisprudence on these aspects of misuse of power that may lead to inequality between the parties in the arbitral process deals with both (1) the obtaining of evidence by improper means and (2) the misuse of the criminal process to obtain an unfair advantage in the arbitral process. **305**

In cases in which such conduct is found, tribunals must also address the scope of their powers to order an appropriate remedy, whether by way of provisional measures or orders in relation to evidence. **306**

2 *The Tribunal's Powers*

Provisional measures. An ICSID tribunal has power to recommend provisional measures under the conditions of Article 47 of the Convention in order to protect the integrity of its process and prevent the aggravation of the dispute. By ratifying the Convention, a State accepts that the tribunal may do so in an appropriate case even if that may entail some interference with a State's sovereign powers and enforcement duties.[303] This power may be used in order to protect the integrity of parties, witnesses or legal representatives. But the tribunal will not act where the alleged risk is merely potential or hypothetical. It must be imminent.[304] **307**

The Tribunal must balance the duties on the parties of good faith and the objective of the non-aggravation of the dispute, while bearing in mind the need to minimise any intervention in the right of the State to act in the public interest: **308**

> [A]ny party to an arbitration should adhere to some procedural duties, including to conduct itself in good faith; moreover, one can expect from a State to adhere in that very capacity, to at least the same principles and standards, in particular to desist from any conduct in this Arbitration that would be incompatible with the Parties' duty of good faith, to respect equality and not to aggravate the dispute. But this Tribunal must be mindful when issuing

[302] Blair and Gojković 2018; Kolo 2010; Bourgeois et al 2018; Wälde 2010: 161.

[303] *Burlington Resources Inc v Ecuador* (Procedural Order No 1) ICSID Case No ARB/08/5, IIC 379 (2009, Kaufmann-Kohler P, Orrego Vicuña & Stern), [66].

[304] Ibid, [45].

provisional measures not to unduly encroach on the State's sovereignty and activities serving public interests.[305]

309 The International Court of Justice has held that its power to indicate provisional measures may apply to a situation in which a State uses its criminal enforcement powers to seize documents relating to the dispute held by the other Party.[306] '[E]quality of the parties must be preserved when they are involved . . . in the process of settling an international dispute by peaceful means.'[307] Such a party 'would expect to undertake these arbitration proceedings or negotiations without interference by the other party in the preparation and conduct of its case'.[308]

310 International investment tribunals also have power to recommend provisional measures in a situation in which the State uses its criminal enforcement powers to obtain evidence, including where it places witnesses under surveillance or intercepts the communications of counsel or witnesses.[309] Such actions may imperil basic procedural fairness as between the parties. The principle is that:

> [P]arties have an obligation to arbitrate fairly and in good faith and that an arbitral tribunal has the inherent jurisdiction to ensure that this obligation is complied with: this principle applies in all arbitration, including investment arbitration, and to all parties, including States (even in the exercise of their sovereign powers).[310]

311 These basic procedural duties constitute obligations of States in international law, which engage the responsibility of the State for the acts of all of its organs and institutions.[311] In this context, a Tribunal has emphasised 'the particular importance of procedural equality between the parties in an arbitration proceeding and that all parties can use and rely on the same evidence'.[312]

312 *Evidentiary powers.* The tribunal retains the inherent power to maintain the equality of the parties by ensuring that a State does not obtain an unfair advantage by gathering evidence through use of its police powers. It may therefore require a respondent to make application to the tribunal before deploying any evidence obtained in the course of a criminal

305 *Caratube International Oil Co LLP v Kazakhstan (Caratube II)* (Decision on Provisional Measures) ICSID Case No ARB/13/13 (2014, Lévy P, Aynès & Salès), [121] (internal citation omitted).

306 *Seizure and Detention of Certain Documents and Data (Timor-Leste v Australia)* (Provisional Measures) [2014] ICJ Rep 147.

307 Ibid, 153, [27].

308 Idem.

309 *Libananco Holdings Co Ltd v Turkey* (Decision on Preliminary Issues) ICSID Case No ARB/06/8, IIC 327 (2008, Hwang P, Álvarez & Berman).

310 Ibid, [78].

311 *Caratube International Oil Co LLP v Kazakhstan (Caratube I)* (Decision on Provisional Measures) ICSID Case No ARB/08/12 (2009, Böckstiegel P, Griffith & Hossain), [118].

312 Ibid, [100].

investigation in the arbitration. In this way, the claimant is afforded the opportunity to be heard on any objections that it may have before the evidence is introduced.[313]

The appropriate remedy where such actions are found will depend upon the nature of the State's actions, the material obtained and its consequences vis-à-vis the maintenance of the integrity of the tribunal's process. **313**

So far as documentary evidence is concerned: **314**

(1) Where the material consists of confidential and privileged communications, it will be excluded from the proceedings; its confidentiality may also need to be protected by an undertaking or placed under seal.[314]
(2) Where the State has obtained documents that would otherwise be admissible in the proceedings, it may be possible to deal with the matter by way of an undertaking to preserve all such evidence and make it available to both parties.[315]
(3) Documents lawfully obtained by a regulator for the purposes of an antitrust investigation will be excluded as evidence in the proceedings.[316]
(4) Where the police seize documents and the respondent makes an explicit commitment that the documents will remain intact and available for the proceedings, a tribunal may decide not to order the return of the documents. Where the seized documents were no longer available in the course of the proceedings, the tribunal would be entitled to draw adverse inferences.[317]

In relation to witness evidence: **315**

(1) Where a witness has been under surveillance, tribunals have accepted undertakings to cease and not to use any of the material so obtained in the arbitration.[318]
(2) Where the State has demanded that a witness produce evidence under threat of prosecution, a Tribunal ordered the State to take no further action on its demand.[319]

313 Ibid, [81]–[82].
314 *Seizure and Detention of Certain Documents* [2014] ICJ Rep 147, 160, [51].
315 *Caratube I*, [100].
316 *Glencore International AG and CI Prodeco SA v Colombia* (Award) ICSID Case No ARB/16/6, IIC 1596 (2019, Fernández-Armesto P, Garibaldi & Thomas), [89]–[90]. The Tribunal clarified that the proper procedure for obtaining evidence was through the agreed document production exercise and Colombia was ordered to resubmit its Counter-Memorial free of references to the disputed documents and without attaching them: [648]–[649].
317 *Gerald International Ltd v Sierra Leone* (Procedural Order No 2, Decision on the Claimant's Request for Provisional Measures) ICSID Case No ARB/19/31 (2020, Reinisch P, Adekoya & Santiago Tawil), [213]–[215].
318 *Europe Cement Investment & Trade SA Claimant v Turkey* (Award) ICSID Case No ARB(AF)/07/2, IIC 385 (2009, McRae P, Lévy & Lew), [35]; see also *Cementownia 'Nowa Huta' SA v Turkey* (Award) ICSID Case No ARB(AF)/06/2, IIC 390 (2009, Tercier P, Lalonde & Thomas), [44].
319 *von Pezold v Zimbabwe* (Provisional Measures Directions) ICSID Case Nos ARB10/15 and ARB10/25, IIC 549 (2012, Fortier P, Chen & Williams), [8].

(3) Where a witness had submitted a statement voluntarily, but was unable to attend the hearing in view of a local court injunction subsequently issued on the application of the respondent, an Annulment Committee found that the tribunal was entitled to receive and consider the statement and did not thereby commit any breach of the principle of the equality of the parties.[320]

(4) Where witnesses declined to appear following the respondent's pursuit of a criminal complaint against them shortly before the hearing, the Tribunal admitted their written statements onto the record (while noting the impact that this would have on the weight that could be accorded to their testimony).[321]

(5) Where a claimant alleged that one of its experts had withdrawn from the proceedings following intimidation by the respondent and the respondent, denying this allegation, sought a declaration that the relevant portion of the expert report be declared inadmissible, the Tribunal decided that the PCA would request the expert to appear.[322]

3 *Criminal Proceedings*

316 Paragraphs (3) and (4) deal in particular with the tribunal's power to recommend provisional measures 'concerning the effect of the exercise of [the State's] powers of criminal investigation and prosecution upon the tribunal's own process'.

317 The institution of criminal proceedings does not in itself threaten the exclusivity of ICSID proceedings:

> Criminal proceedings deal with criminal liability and not with investment disputes, and fall by definition outside the scope of the Centre's jurisdiction and the competence of this Tribunal. Neither the ICSID Convention nor the BIT contain any rule enjoining the State from exercising criminal jurisdiction, nor do they exempt suspected criminals from prosecution by virtue of their being investors.[323]

318 In exceptional cases, investment tribunals have recommended provisional measures to restrain the pursuit of criminal investigations or prosecutions.[324] There must be a close link between the criminal proceedings and the fair conduct of the arbitration.[325] A tribunal will not exercise its powers in this respect where the alleged risk is only a potential one; it

320 *Enron Creditors Recovery Corporation v Argentina* (Decision on Annulment) ICSID Case No ARB/01/3, IIC 441 (2010, Griffith P, Robinson & Tresselt), [176]–[178].

321 *Ruby Roz Agricol LLP v Kazakhstan* (Award on Jurisdiction) UNCITRAL, IIC 602 (2013) (Redfern P, Boesch & Neuhaus), [136].

322 *Guaracachi America Inc and Rurelec Plc v Bolivia* (Procedural Order No 16) PCA 2011–17 (2013, Miguel Júdice P, Conthe & Vinuesa), [7]–[8].

323 *Quiborax SA v Bolivia* (Decision on Provisional Measures) ICSID Case No ARB/06/2, IIC 422 (2010, Kaufmann-Kohler P, Lalonde & Stern), [129].

324 *City Oriente Ltd v Ecuador* (Decision on Provisional Measures) ICSID Case No ARB/06/21, IIC 309 (2007 Fernández-Armesto P, Grigera Naón & Thomas); *Gerald International*, [147], [195]–[205].

325 *Seizure and Detention of Certain Documents* [2014] ICJ Rep 147, 152, [23]; *Quiborax*, [120]–[121].

must be imminent.[326] A 'particularly high threshold must be overcome before an ICSID tribunal can indeed recommend provisional measures regarding criminal investigations conducted by a state'.[327] A State has a sovereign right to police breaches of its own criminal law within its territory through its own criminal procedures.

In order to obtain provisional measures, the claimant has to establish that the respondent's investigations were preventing them from asserting their rights in the arbitration, causing them irreparable and imminent harm requiring urgent relief. The claimant must also establish 'that there is no higher or equivalent public interest of the State to be a party to the criminal proceedings'.[328] **319**

Such instances will always be exceptional. In one case, the claimant submitted that the respondent was 'using the process of the criminal law to obtain an unfair advantage in the arbitration proceedings over the Claimant, aggravating the inequality of arms between the parties'. The Tribunal granted the application, noting that the Respondent's full-scale criminal investigation launched shortly before the merits hearing in the arbitration would be highly disruptive of the Claimant's ability to prepare and present its case.[329] **320**

In another case, the Tribunal found that criminal proceedings appeared to be part of a defence strategy adopted by the State for the purpose of the arbitration.[330] The Tribunal found there was a threat to the procedural integrity of the proceedings, in particular, with respect to their right to access to evidence through potential witnesses.[331] The harm that such a stay would cause to the respondent was proportionately less than the harm caused to claimants if the criminal proceedings were not stayed until the conclusion of the arbitration.[332] **321**

The high threshold that applies before a tribunal will recommend any measures in relation to criminal proceedings means that the application will not succeed unless it is supported by clear evidence.[333] **322**

326 *Ipek Investment Ltd v Turkey* (Procedural Order No 5 Claimant's Request for Provisional Measures) ICSID Case No ARB/18/18 (2019, McLachlan P, Fortier & Lévy), [43].

327 *Caratube I*, [137]; *Teinver SA v Argentina* (Decision on Provisional Measures) ICSID Case No ARB/09/1 (2016, Buergenthal P, Alvarez & Hossain).

328 *Caratube II*, [135]; *Hydro Srl v Albania* (Order on Provisional Measures) ICSID Case No ARB/15/28 (2016, Pryles P, Glick & Poncet).

329 *Lao Holdings NV v Laos* (Decision on Provisional Measures) ICSID Case No ARB(AF)/12/6, IIC 646 (2014, Binnie P, Hanotiau & Stern), [39]–[40].

330 *Quiborax*, [122].

331 Ibid, [148].

332 Ibid, [163]–[165].

333 *Churchill Mining Plc and Planet Mining Pty Ltd v Indonesia* (Procedural Order No 14 Provisional Measures) ICSID Case Nos ARB/12/14 and ARB/12/40 (2014, Kaufmann-Kohler P, Hwang & van den Berg), [72].

CHAPTER 3: SUBSTANTIVE EQUALITY OF ARMS

ARTICLE 12:

Costs

(1) The ability of parties, whether investors or States, to pursue or defend claims before a tribunal should not be determined on grounds of cost. Particular regard should be paid in this context to the position of small and medium-sized enterprises and to that of developing States.

(2) Where a party's pursuit of its claim or defence is supported by third party funding, that party shall disclose the identity of the third party funder, so that the tribunal may consider, inter alia, any possible implications for the maintenance of the impartiality of the tribunal.

(3) Where on application the tribunal is satisfied that a claimant may be unable to pay an award of costs in the event that its claim is unsuccessful and that the provision of security is necessary to preserve the equal protection of the parties, the tribunal has discretion to order security for costs.

323 The final aspect of the equality principle considered in the resolution concerns the circumstances in which an international investment tribunal may properly recognise the fact that the parties' right to equality of arms may be materially affected by an inequality of financial resources available to devote to the pursuit or defence of the claim.[334]

324 This consideration may, depending on the circumstances, apply both to claimants and to respondents:

(1) One valuable attribute of arbitration pursuant to the standing consent of a State given by treaty is that it opens access to a neutral forum for the resolution of investment dispute to all investors – small as well as large – irrespective of whether they might otherwise have been able to negotiate a concession contract with the State containing an arbitration agreement. '[I]t was not the intent of the drafters of the ICSID Convention to exclude claimants advancing claims of minor financial dimension.'[335] In practice, there is evidence of concern 'that the accessibility to the ISDS mechanism remains *de facto* a prerogative mainly of large-scale firms, as its costs and complexity make it difficult for small private investors to resort to it'.[336]

(2) At the same time, many large claimants may have access to resources in the pursuit of their claims that outweigh those of States – especially small or least developed States. A significant impetus to reform of the current system has been the concern of States at

[334] Bain 2018: 291; Treves 2015; Wälde 2007: 43, 54.

[335] *Malaysian Historical Salvors Sdn Bhd v Malaysia* (Decision on Annulment) ICSID Case No ARB/05/10, IIC 372 (2009, Schwebel P, Tomka & Shahabuddeen (dissenting)), [82].

[336] EC 2015: 16; EU Council 2018: [17]. See also Franck 2019: 190.

excessively burdensome costs incurred in defending such cases, especially for the poorest States.[337]

The requirement of equality of treatment does not preclude the tribunal from taking into account objective factors that may affect the ability of a party to participate equally in the proceeding. So far as possible, it is mandated to secure equality in substance, not merely in form. This consideration may apply, in particular, to small and medium-sized enterprise claimants and to developing States, particularly least-developed States. ICSID tribunals have taken such considerations into account in their procedural orders.[338] These considerations are also an important feature of the negotiations for an International Tribunal for Investments.[339] Some consideration is being given to the possibility of establishing an advisory centre for investment claims, on the analogy of the Advisory Centre on WTO Law.[340] **325**

In practice, the different economic position of the parties most commonly arises for consideration by tribunals in the context of their exercise of their powers to award costs, together with the related questions of third-party funding and the possibility of making orders for security for costs. It is to these questions that Article 12 is devoted. **326**

1 *Costs*

The most significant element in the parties' costs is generally the fees incurred for legal representation. The parties have the freedom to appoint counsel of their choice. **327**

The principal mechanism available to a tribunal to mitigate any costs burden is through its allocation of costs, either through an interim decision[341] or in its final award. For this latter purpose, an ICSID tribunal is obliged to assess the parties' expenses and has wide discretion to 'decide how and by whom those expenses ... shall be paid.'[342] Proposed Arbitration Rule 3(1) introduces a general duty on both the tribunal and the parties to conduct the proceeding in good faith and in an expeditious and cost-effective **328**

337 EU Council 2018: [16]; UNCTAD 2013: 4.

338 *Amco Asia Corporation v Indonesia* (Decision on Annulment) 1 ICSID Rep 509 (1986, Seidl-Hohenveldern P, Feliciano & Giardina), [90]; *SARL Benvenuti & Bonfant v Congo* (Award) 1 ICSID Rep 335 (1980, Trolle P, Bystricky & Razafindralambo), [1.29], [1.33]; *Zhinvali Development Ltd v Georgia* (Award) ICSID Case No ARB/00/1, 10 ICSID Rep 3 (2003, Robinson P, Rubin & Jacovides), [30]–[33]. Cf. WTO DSU, where recognition of the equality of the parties did not preclude the adoption of special and differential treatment for developing country members: arts 3(12) (different procedure available to developing country complainants), 4(10) (special attention to the needs of developing country Members during consultations), 8(10) (ability to request one panellist for a developing country), 12(10) (longer time periods for consultation and sufficient time to prepare case) and 27 (assistance to developing country Members by the Secretariat in preparing their case).

339 EU Council 2018: [16]–[17].

340 Bungenberg and Reinisch 2019: [4.1.8]; Sauvant 2019; Schwieder 2018; UNCITRAL 2019c, UN Doc A/CN.9/WG.III/WP.168.

341 ICSID Arbitration Rule 28(1).

342 Art 61(2).

manner.[343] Proposed Arbitration Rule 52 would require the tribunal to consider all relevant circumstances including the outcome of the proceeding or any part of it and the conduct of the parties during the proceeding.[344]

329 In practice, in the absence of specific reasons to decide otherwise, ICSID tribunals and annulment committees have frequently (though not invariably) divided the fees and expenses of the tribunal and the charges for the use of the Centre equally and have left each party to bear its own legal fees.[345] This approach can 'discourage if not debar small claims.'[346] By the same token, the absence of a risk that a claimant might have to bear the respondent's costs as well as its own if unsuccessful can also encourage unmeritorious actions.[347]

330 The UNCITRAL Rules start from the position that the loser should pay, providing:

> The costs of the arbitration shall in principle be borne by the unsuccessful party or parties. However, the arbitral tribunal may apportion each of such costs between the parties if it determines that apportionment is reasonable, taking into account the circumstances of the case.[348]

331 The same position (limited to recovery of 'reasonable costs') is now adopted in the EU model for an International Tribunal for Investments.[349]

2 *Third-Party Funding*

332 Paragraphs (2) and (3) of Article 12 deal with two distinct but related issues that may affect the substantive equality of arms in relation to costs:

(1) the provision of third-party litigation funding (paragraph (2));[350] and
(2) the provision of security for costs (paragraph (3)).[351]

333 Resort to third-party funding can have implications for arbitrator impartiality. This issue of potential conflicts of interest has now been widely acknowledged by the arbitration community and has recently been addressed in the 2014 revisions of the IBA Guidelines on Conflicts of Interest in International Arbitration. The IBA Guidelines now specifically

343 ICSID 2020b: 33.
344 Ibid, 57.
345 Schreuer et al 2009: 1236.
346 *Malaysian Historical Salvors*, [82].
347 Schreuer, 1229.
348 Art 42(1), UNCITRAL Rules 2010.
349 Art 28(4), EU TTIP Proposal 2015; Art 8.39(5), CETA.
350 De Brabandere and Lepeltak 2012; ICCA 2018: ch 8.
351 *RSM Production Corporation v Saint Lucia* (Decision on Security for Costs) ICSID Case No ARB/12/10 (2014, Elsing P, Griffith & Nottingham).

provide that a funder may be considered the 'equivalent of the party' for conflicts.[352] General Standard 6(b) provides that: 'If one of the parties is a legal entity, any legal or physical person having a controlling influence on the legal entity, or a direct economic interest in, or a duty to indemnify a party for, the award to be rendered in the arbitration, may be considered to bear the identity of such party.'[353]

The 2020 draft amendments to the ICSID Arbitration Rules propose mandatory disclosure of the identity of a third-party funder. The draft Rule defines third-party funding as derived from: **334**

> . . . any non-party from which the party, directly or indirectly, has received funds for the pursuit or defense of the proceeding through a donation or grant, or in return for remuneration dependent on the outcome of the proceeding.[354]

A similar provision is already included in several recently concluded EU investment treaties.[355] Other institutional rules also confer an express power on the tribunal to order disclosure of a third-party funder.[356]

Paragraph (2) adopts this approach, requiring disclosure of the identity of the third-party funder 'so that the tribunal may consider, inter alia, any possible implications for the maintenance of the impartiality of the tribunal'. **335**

3 *Security for Costs*

The general approach adopted by investment tribunals to date has been that security for costs should be awarded only in exceptional circumstances.[357] Accordingly, orders for security for costs are 'extremely rare'.[358] One Tribunal has recently held that neither a party's impecuniousity or its reliance on third party, in and of itself, is, alone, sufficient to meet the exceptional circumstances standard, noting that 'One reason is that a claimant may be able to prove on the merits that the respondent wrongfully caused its financial difficulty.'[359] **336**

352 IBA 2014: 14.

353 Ibid, 13. See: *Çap & Sehil Inşaat Endustri ve Ticaret Ltd Sti v Turkmenistan* (Procedural Order No 3) ICSID No ARB/12/6 (2015, Lew P, Boisson de Chazournes & Hanotiau), [9]; Darwazeh and Leleu 2016: 132–3; Frignati 2016.

354 Draft Arbitration Rule 14, ICSID 2020b: 37.

355 See, e.g., Art 8.26, CETA; Ch 3, Art 3.37, EU–Vietnam Investment Protection Agreement.

356 Rule 24, SIAC Investment Arbitration Rules 2017; Art 27, CIETAC International Investment Arbitration Rules 2017.

357 *Adamakopoulos v Cyprus* (Decision on Jurisdiction) ICSID Case No ARB/15/49 (2020, McRae P, Kohen & Escobar), [264]; *Tennant Energy LLC v Canada* (Procedural Order No 4) PCA Case No 2018–54 (2020, Bull P, Doak Bishop & Bethlehem), [173], in particular, noting that the high threshold is 'not surprising, given that security for costs orders raise specific access to justice issues that do not arise with other forms of provisional relief'.

358 *Dirk Herzig as Insolvency Administrator over the Assets of Unionmatex Industrieanlagen GmbH v Turkmenistan* (Decision on the Respondent's Request for Security for Costs and the Claimant's Request for Security for Claim) ICSID Case No ARB/18/35 (2020, Reed P, Sands & Voser), [50].

359 Ibid, [54]–[55].

337 A Tribunal recently considered "whether a party's impecunity plus reliance on third-party funding, taken together, comprise the exceptional circumstances warranting an order for security for costs.'[360] A majority in that case concluded that the Respondent would be unduly prejudiced without an order for security for costs.[361] The Tribunal readily accepted the Claimant's argument that his reliance on third-party funding was not sufficient, in and of itself, to meet the exceptional circumstances standard.[362]

338 The draft amendments to the ICSID Arbitration Rules propose making express provision for the power of tribunal to order security for costs. This would require the tribunal to consider a party's ability or willingness to comply with an adverse order as to costs and any other relevant circumstances.[363] The Report notes that one of the arguments in favour of a power to order security is that it may balance the position of the parties both in the pursuit of the claim and in the enforceability of an award. On the other hand, care must be taken not to allow the provision of security to deter meritorious claims.[364] The existence of third-party funding is a factor that a tribunal may take into account when assessing whether to order a party to put up security for costs, but is not on its own dispositive.[365] The Convention provides no equivalent provision enabling a claimant to obtain provisional measures to secure eventual payment on an award.[366]

339 If the claimant is impecunious and supported by a third-party funder, another possible route to control costs has been the development of a power of tribunals to order such a funder to meet the respondent's costs if the claim is not successful.[367] In some cases, the terms of funding may include litigation insurance that would cover an adverse award of costs.[368]

340 Paragraph (3) confirms that the tribunal has discretion to order security for costs '[w]here on application the tribunal is satisfied that a claimant may be unable to pay an award of costs in the event that its claim is unsuccessful and that the provision of security is necessary to preserve the equal protection of the parties.'

360 Ibid, [56].
361 Ibid, [63].
362 Ibid, [54].
363 Draft Arbitration Rule 53(3).
364 ICSID 2018a: vol 3, 230, [497]–[498].
365 Draft Arbitration Rule 53(4); *Armas v Venezuela* (Procedural Order No 9, Decision on Provisional Measures) PCA Case No 2016–08, IIC 1457 (2018, Nunes Pinto P, Gómez-Pinzón & Torres Bernárdez); *Tennant Energy LLC v Canada* (Procedural Order No 4) PCA Case No 2018–54 (2020, Bull P, Doak Bishop & Bethlehem), [109]. See also Hoffmann 2018.
366 *Eskosol SPA in liquidazione v Italy* (Decision on Respondent's Request for Provisional Measures) ICSID No ARB/15/50 (2017, Kalicki P, Stern & Santiago Tawil), [35], citing *Burimi SRL & Eagle Games SHA v Albania* (Procedural Order No 2) ICSID No ARB/11/18 (2012, Price P, Cremades & Fadlallah), [49]: 'The Tribunal acknowledges that non-payment of awards of damages or costs by respondents and claimants poses a systemic risk to the arbitration of international investment disputes.'
367 Honlet 2015.
368 *Eskosol*, [37]. In *Dirk Herzig*, the Claimant made a request for security for claim. The majority of the Tribunal did not accept the Claimant's arguments based on equality of treatment, in light of the disproportionate nature and amount involved in security for one party's costs and in security for one party's total damages and costs. The Tribunal also noted that to the best of its knowledge an order for security for claim is unprecedented, and for good reason: see [68].

Books and Articles

Al-Khasawneh, A 2015. 'Foreword', in A Savarian, F Fontanelli, R Baker and V Tsevelekos (eds), *Procedural Fairness in International Courts and Tribunals* (London: British Institute of International and Comparative Law)

Alexandrov, S A and Carlson, M 2010. 'The Opportunity to Be Heard: Accommodating Amicus Curiae Participation in Investment Treaty Arbitration', in D Arias and M Fernández-Ballesteros (eds), *Liber Amicorum: Bernardo Cremades* (Madrid: La Ley)

Amado, J, Kern, J and Rodríguez, M 2018. *Arbitrating the Conduct of International Investors* (Cambridge University Press)

Antonopoulos, C 2011. *Counterclaims before the International Court of Justice* (The Hague: TMC Asser Press)

Atanansova, D, Benoit, A M and Ostransky, J 2014. 'Legal Framework for Counterclaims in Investment Treaty Arbitration' 31 J Int'l Arb 357

Bain, E 2018. 'When Some Are More Equal than Others: The Need for a More Substantive Conception of "Equality of the Parties" in Investment Arbitration', in *Yearbook on International Investment Law and Policy 2015–2016* (New York: Oxford University Press)

Bantekas, I 2020a. 'Equal Treatment of Parties in International Commercial Arbitration' 69 ICLQ 991

—2020b. 'Article 18: Equal Treatment of Parties', in I Bantekas, P Ortolani, S Ali, M A Gomez and M Polkinghome (eds), *UNCITRAL Model Law on International Commercial Arbitration: A Commentary* (Cambridge University Press)

Beechey, J 2019. 'The Pandora's Box of Third-Party Funding: Some Practical Suggestions for Arbitrators in Light of Recent Developments' 20 ICCA Congress Series 558

Berger, K P and Jensen, J O 2016. 'Due Process Paranoia and the Procedural Judgment Rule: A Safe Harbour for Procedural Management Decisions by International Arbitrators' 32 Arb Int'l 415

Bernadini, P 2017. 'Reforming Investor–State Dispute Settlement: The Need to Balance Both Parties' Interests' 32 ICSID Rev – FILJ 38

Bishop, R D, Crawford, J and Reisman, W M 2014. *Foreign Investment Disputes: Cases, Materials and Commentary*, 2nd edn (Alphen aan den Rijn: Kluwer Law International)

Blair, C and Gojković, E V 2018. 'WikiLeaks and Beyond: Discerning an International Standard for the Admissibility of Illegally Obtained Evidence' 33 ICSID Rev – FILJ 235

Boisson de Chazournes, L 2018. 'Changes in the Balance of Rights and Obligations: Towards Investor Responsibilization', in T El Ghadban, C Mazuy and A Senegacnik (eds), *La Protection des investissements étrangers, vers une reaffirmation de l'Etat? Actes du colloque du 2 juin 2017* (Paris: Pedone)

—2015. 'Transparency in Investor–State Arbitration: An Incremental Approach' 2 BCDR Int'l Arb Rev 59

—2005. 'Making the Proceedings Public and Allowing Third-Party Interventions: Are the New Generation Bilateral Investment Treaties (US, Canada) Bifurcating Investment Arbitration from International Commercial Arbitration?' 6 JWIT 105

—2004. 'Transparency and "Amicus Curiae" Briefs' 5 JWIT 333

Boisson de Chazournes, L, Bonnin, V, Kaufmann-Kohler, G and Mbengue, M M 2006. 'Consolidation of Proceedings in Investment Arbitration: How Can Multiple Proceedings Arising from the Same or Related Situations Be Handled Efficiently?' Final Report on the Geneva Colloquium held on 22 April 2006, 21 ICSID Rev – FILJ 59

Boisson de Chazournes, L and Mbengue, M M 2003. 'The Amici Curiae and the WTO Dispute Settlement System: The Doors Are Open' 2 LPICT 205

Bonnitcha, J, Poulsen, L and Waibel, M, 2017. *The Political Economy of the Investment Treaty Regime* (Oxford University Press)

Boon, K E 2018. 'Investment Treaty Arbitration: Making a Place for Small Claims' 19 JWIT 667

Born, G 2014. *International Commercial Arbitration*, 2nd edn (Alphen aan den Rijn:Kluwer)

—2011. 'The US Supreme Court and Class Action Arbitration: A Tragedy of Errors' (1 July), www.kluwerarbitrationblog.com

—2009. *International Commercial Arbitration*, 1st edn (Alphen aan den Rijn: Kluwer)

Bottini, G, Titi, C, Pérez-Aznar, F, Chaisse, J, Jovanovic, M and Puigdemont Sola, O 2020. 'Excessive Costs and Recoverability of Costs Awards in Investment Arbitration' 21 JWIT 251

Bourgeois, V, Eyskens, W, Fernandez-Bertier, M and Stoyanov, M 2018. 'Procedural Interplay between Investment Arbitration and Criminal Proceedings in the Context of Corruption Allegations' Belgian Review of Arbitration 7

Broches, A 1972. 'The Convention on the Settlement of Investment Disputes between States and Nationals of Other States' 136 Recueil des *Cours* 331

Bronckers, M 2015. 'Is Investor–State Dispute Settlement (ISDS) Superior to Litigation before Domestic Courts?' 18 JIEL 655

Brower, C N and Kumar, S P 2015. 'Investomercial Arbitration: Whence Cometh It? What Is It? Whither Goeth It?' 30 ICSID Rev – FILJ 35

Brower, C N and Rosenberg, C B 2013. 'The Death of the Two-Headed Nightingale: Why the Paulsson-van den Berg Presumption that Party-Appointed Arbitrators Are Untrustworthy Is Wrongheaded' 29 Arb Int'l 7

Brown de Vejar, K and Baldwin, C 2019. 'The Economics of Access: Systemic Imbalances in ISDS' 20 ICCA Congress Series 520

Bubrowski, H 2013. 'Balancing IIA Arbitration through the Use of Counterclaims', in A de Mestral and C Lévesque (eds), *Improving International Investment Agreements* (Abingdon: Routledge)

Bungenberg, M and Reinisch, A 2019. 'Design and Implementation of a Two-Tiered MIC', in *From Bilateral Arbitral Tribunals and Investment Courts to a Multilateral Investment Court: Options Regarding the Institutionalization of Investor–State Dispute Settlement*, European Yearbook of International Economic Law Series, 2nd edn (Berlin: Springer)

Carlston, K 1946. *The Process of International Arbitration* (New York: Columbia University Press)

Caron, D and Caplan, L 2013. *The UNCITRAL Arbitration Rules: A Commentary*, 2nd edn (Oxford University Press)

Chaisse, J, Choukroune L and Jusoh, S (eds) 2020. *Handbook of International Investment Law and Policy* (Singapore: Springer)

Chaisse, J and Sejko, D 2016. 'Investor–State Arbitration Distorted: When the Claimant Is a State', in L Choukroune (ed), *Judging the State in International Trade and Investment Law: Sovereignty Modern, the Law and the Economics* (Singapore: Springer)

Cheng, B 1953. *General Principles of Law as Applied by International Courts and Tribunals* (London: Stevens)

Cleis, M N 2017. *The Independence and Impartiality of ICSID Arbitrators: Current Case Law, Alternative Approaches, and Improvement Suggestions* (Leiden: Brill Nijhoff)

Lord Collins (gen ed), 2012. *Dicey, Morris & Collins on the Conflict of Laws*, 15th edn (London: Sweet & Maxwell)

Crawford, J R 2015. 'Challenges to Arbitrators in ICSID Arbitration', in D Caron, S W Schill, A Cohen Smutny and E E Triantafilou (eds), *Practising Virtue: Inside International Arbitration* (Oxford University Press)

—2017. 'The Ideal Arbitrator: Does One Size Fit All?' 32 Am U Int'l LR 1003

Croft, C, Kee, C and Waincymer, J 2013. *A Guide to the UNCITRAL Arbitration Rules* (Cambridge University Press)

Darwazeh, N and Leleu, A 2016. 'Disclosure and Security for Costs or How to Address Imbalances Created by Third-Party Funding' 33 J Int'l Arb 125

De Brabandere, E 2012. 'Individuals in Advisory Proceedings before the International Court of Justice: Equality of the Parties and the Court's Discretionary Authority' 11 LPICT 253

De Brabandere, E and Lepeltak, J 2012. 'Third-Party Funding in International Investment Arbitration' 27 ICSID Rev – FILJ 379

De Nanteuil, A 2018. 'Counterclaims in Investment Arbitration: Old Questions, New Answers?' 17 LPICT 374

Della Cananea, G 2016. '*Audi alteram partem*' in *Due Process of Law beyond the State* (Oxford University Press)

Di Rosa, P 2019. 'Challenges for Counsel in the Representation of States and State-Owned Entities in International Arbitration: A Practitioner's Perspective' 20 ICCA Congress Series 607

Dolzer, R and Schreuer, C 2012. *Principles of International Investment Law*, 2nd edn (Oxford University Press)

Douglas, Z 2009. *The International Law of Investment Claims* (Cambridge University Press)

El-Hosseny, F 2018. *Civil Society in Investment Treaty Arbitration: Status and Prospects* (Leiden: Brill Nijhoff)

European Federation for Investment Law and Arbitration (EFILA) 2015. 'A Response to the Criticism against ISDS' (17 May), http://efila.org/wp-content/uploads/2015/05/EFILA_in_response_to_the-criticism_of_ISDS_final_draft.pdf

Fach Gómez, K 2019. *Key Duties of International Investment Arbitrators: A Transnational Study of Legal and Ethical Dilemmas* (Cham: Springer Nature)

Feldman, M 2016. 'State-Owned Enterprises as Claimants in International Investment Arbitration' 31 ICSID Rev – FILJ 24

Fouret, J, Gerbay R and Alvarez, G M (eds) 2019. *The ICSID Convention, Regulations and Rules: A Practical Commentary* (Cheltenham: Edward Elgar)

Franck, S D 2019. 'Costs – Risks and Reality', in *Arbitration Costs: Myths and Realities in Investment Treaty Arbitration* (Oxford University Press)

Franck, T 1993. 'Fairness in the International Legal and Institutional System' 240 Recueil des Cours 9

Frignati, V 2016. 'Ethical Implications of Third-Party Funding in International Arbitration' 32 Arb Int'l 505

Gaillard, E and Savage, J (eds) 1999. *Fouchard, Gaillard, Goldman on International Commercial Arbitration* (The Hague and Boston, MA: Kluwer Law International)

Giorgetti, C and Dunoff, J L 2019. 'Ex Pluribus Unum? On the Form and Shape of a Common Code of Ethics in International Litigation' 113 AJIL Unbound 312

Giorgetti, C, Ratner, S, Dunoff, J, Hamamoto, S, Nottage, L, Schill, S W and Waibel, M 2020. 'Independence and Impartiality of Adjudicators in Investment Dispute Settlement: Assessing Challenges and Reform Options' 21 JWIT 441

Goh, N 2018. 'The Power of Tribunals to Enjoin Criminal Proceedings: A Widening Power or Converging High Bar?' 33 ICSID Rev – FILJ 88

Gomez-Acebo, A 2019. 'A Special Role of Party-Appointed Arbitrators?' 20 ICCA Congress Series 381

Gottwald, E 2007. 'Leveling the Playing Field: Is It Time for a Legal Assistance Center for Developing Nations in Investment Treaty Arbitration?' 22 Am U Int'l LR 237

Gomula, J 1991. 'The International Court of Justice and Administrative Tribunals of International Organizations' 13 Mich JIL 83

Gross, L 1958. 'Participation of Individuals in Advisory Proceedings before the International Court of Justice: Question of Equality between the Parties' 52 AJIL 16

Hanotiau, B 2020. *Complex Arbitrations: Multi-Party, Multi-Contract, Multi-Issue – A Comparative Study*, 2nd edn (Alphen aan den Rijn: Kluwer Law International)

Hepburn, J and Kabra, R 2017. 'India's New Model BIT: Fit for Purpose?' 1 Indian LR 95

Hoffmann, A 2018. 'The Impact of Third-Party Funding on an ICSID Tribunal's Decision on Security for Costs', in M Akbaba and G Capurro (eds), *International Challenges in Investment Arbitration* (New York: Routledge)

Honlet, J C 2015. 'Recent Decisions on Third-Party Funding in Investment Arbitration' 30 ICSID Rev – FILJ 699

Ishikawa, T 2019. 'Counterclaims and the Rule of Law in Investment Arbitration' 113 AJIL Unbound 33

Kaeckenbeeck, G S 1946. 'Upper Silesia under the League of Nations' 243 Annals AAPSS 129

Kao, C 2019. 'Assessing the Rules of Appointing Arbitrators under the EU's Investment Court System' 27 Eur Rev 210

Kaufmann-Kohler, G and Potestà, M 2020. *Investor–State Dispute Settlement and National Courts: Current Framework and Reform Options*, European Yearbook of International Economic Law (Cham: Springer)

Kazazi, M 1995. *Burden of Proof and Related Issues: A Study on Evidence before International Tribunals* (The Hague, London and Boston: Kluwer)

Kessedjian, C 2020. 'Le tiers impartial et indépendant en droit international: Juge, arbitre, médiateur, conciliateur' 403 Recueil des Cours 49

Kho, S, Yanovich, A, Casey, B and Strauss, J 2017. 'The EU TTIP Investment Court Proposal and the WTO Dispute Settlement System' 32 ICSID Rev – FILJ 326

Kohen, M and Dumberry, P 2019. *The Institute of International Law's Resolution on State Succession and State Responsibility: Introduction, Text and Commentaries* (Cambridge University Press)

Kolb, R 2013. *The International Court of Justice* (Oxford and Portland, OR: Hart)

Kolo, A 2010. 'Witness Intimidation, Tampering and Other Related Abuses of Process in Investment Arbitration: Possible Remedies Available to the Arbitral Tribunal' 26 Arb Int'l 43

Kotuby, C and Sobota, L 2017. *General Principles of Law and International Due Process* (Oxford University Press)

Jennings, R and Watts, A (eds) 1992. *Oppenheim's International Law*, 9th edn (Oxford University Press), vol 1

Lalive, P and Halonen, L 2011. 'On the Availability of Counterclaims in Investment Treaty Arbitration' II Czech YBIL 141

Lauterpacht, H 1933. *The Function of Law in the International Community* (Oxford University Press)

Lixinski, L 2015. 'The Right to a Competent Judge: Selecting, Training and Assigning International Criminal Judges', in A Savarian, F Fontanelli, R Baker and V Tsevelekos (eds), *Procedural Fairness in International Courts and Tribunals* (London: British Institute of International and Comparative Law)

Luttrell, S 2016. 'Testing the ICSID Framework for Arbitrator Challenges' 31 ICSID Rev – FILJ 597

Mackenzie, R, Malleson, K, Martin, P and Sands, P 2010. *Selecting International Judges: Principle, Process and Politics* (Oxford University Press)

Malmström, C (European Commissioner for Trade) 2017. 'Reforming Investment Dispute Settlement' (27 February), http://trade.ec.europa.eu/doclib/docs/2017/february/tradoc_155393.pdf

Mani, V S 1980. *International Adjudication: Procedural Aspects* (The Hague, London and Boston, MA: Martinus Nijhoff)

Mbengue, M M and Schacherer, S 2018. 'Africa and the Rethinking of International Investment Law: About the Elaboration of the Pan-African Investment Code', in

A Roberts, P B Stephan, P-H Verdier and M Versteeg (eds), *Comparative International Law* (Oxford University Press)

McLachlan, C, Shore, L and Weiniger, M 2017. *International Investment Arbitration: Substantive Principles*, 2nd edn (Oxford University Press)

Mikhailovich Khodykin, R, Mulcahy, C and Martin Fletcher, N H 2019. *A Guide to the IBA Rules on the Taking of Evidence in International Arbitration* (Oxford University Press)

Moseley, S E 2019. 'Disclosing Third-Party Funding in International Investment Arbitration' 97 Texas LR 1181

Onyema, E 2019. 'African Participation in the ICSID System: Appointment and Disqualification of Arbitrators' 34 ICSID Rev – FILJ 365

Parlett, K 2011. *The Individual in the International Legal System: Continuity and Change in International Law* (Cambridge University Press)

Paulsson, J 2013. *The Idea of Arbitration* (Oxford University Press)

Pellet, A 2012. 'Judicial Settlement of International Disputes', in R Wolfrum (ed), *Max Planck Encyclopaedia of Public International Law* (Oxford University Press)

Polanco, R 2019. *The Return of the Home State to Investor–State Disputes: Bringing Back Diplomatic Protection?* (Cambridge University Press)

Poudret, J-F and Besson, S 2007. *Comparative Law of International Commercial Arbitration*, 2nd edn, trans S Berti and A Ponti (London: Sweet & Maxwell)

Poulsen, L N S 2016. 'States as Foreign Investors: Diplomatic Disputes and Legal Fictions' 31 ICSID Rev – FILJ 12

Puig, S and Shaffer, G 2018. 'Imperfect Alternatives: Institutional Choice and the Reform of Investment Law' 112 AJIL 361

Ramesh, S 2020. 'Third-Party Funding in International Arbitration: Ownership of the Claim, Consequences for Costs Orders, and Regulation' 36 Arb Int'l 275

Reed, L 2017. 'Ab(use) of Due Process: Sword vs Shield' 33 Arb Int'l 361

Reinisch, A 2017. 'The European Union and Investor–State Dispute Settlement: From Investor–State Arbitration to a Permanent Investment Court', in A de Mestral (ed), *Second Thoughts: Investor–State Arbitration between Developed Democracies* (Montreal: McGill-Queen's University Press)

Reinisch, A and Knahr, C 2008. 'From the United Nations Administrative Tribunal to the United Nations Appeals Tribunal – Reform of the Administration of Justice System within the United Nations' 12 Max Planck UNYB 447

Reinisch, A and Knahr, C 2007. 'Transparency versus Confidentiality in International Investment Arbitration – The Biwater Gauff Compromise' 6 LPICT 97

Riffel, C 2020. 'Does Investor–State Dispute Settlement Discriminate against Nationals?' 21 German LJ 197

Roberts, A 2018. 'Incremental, Systemic, and Paradigmatic Reform of Investor–State Arbitration' 112 AJIL 410

Sauvant, K P 2019. 'An Advisory Centre on International Investment Law: Key Features' (10 September) Academic Forum on ISDS Concept Paper 2019/14

Sarvarian, A, Fontanelli, F, Baker, R and Tzevelekos, V 2015. *Procedural Fairness in International Courts and Tribunals* (London: British Institute of International and Comparative Law)

Schabas, W 2015. *The European Convention on Human Rights: A Commentary* (Oxford University Press)

Schneiderman, D 2017. 'Listening to Investors (and Others): Audi Alteram Partem and the Future of International Investment Law', in A de Mestral (ed), *Second Thoughts: Investor State Arbitration between Developed Democracies* (Montreal: McGill-Queen's University Press)

Schreuer, C, Malintoppi, L, Reinisch, A and Sinclair, A 2009. *The ICSID Convention: A Commentary*, 2nd edn (Cambridge University Press)

Schwebel, S M 2016. 'The Proposals of the European Commission for Investment Protection and an Investment Court System' (17 May), http://isdsblog.com/wp-content/uploads/sites/2/2016/05/THEPROPOSALSOFTHEEUROPEANCOMMISSION.pdf

—1999. 'National Judges and Judges Ad Hoc of the International Court of Justice' 48 ICLQ 889

Schwieder, R W 2018. 'Legal Aid and Investment Treaty Disputes: Lessons Learned from the Advisory Centre on WTO Law and Investment Experiences' 19 JWIT 628

Semertzi, A 2014. 'The Preclusion of Direct Effect in the Recently Concluded EU Free Trade Agreements' 51 CMLR 1125

Sharpe, J K and Jacob, M 2018. 'Counterclaims and State Claims', in C L Beharry (ed), *Contemporary and Emerging Issues on the Law of Damages and Valuation in International Investment Arbitration* (Leiden: Brill Nijhoff)

Shaw Kern, J 2019. 'Investor Responsibility as Familiar Frontier' 113 AJIL Unbound 28

Sheppard, A 2016. 'The Approach of Investment Treaty Tribunals to Evidentiary Privileges' 31 ICSID Rev – FILJ 670

Sourgens, F G, Duggal, K and Laird, I A, 2018. *Evidence in International Investment Arbitration* (Oxford University Press)

Steingruber, A 2021. 'Counterclaims: A Critical Analysis of Article 6 of the 2019 The Hague Resolution of the Institut de Droit International on the "Equality of Parties before International Investment Tribunals"' 41 ICSID Rev – FILJ, doi: 10.1093/icsidreview/siaa038

Stern, B 2009. 'Are Some Issues Too Political to Be Arbitrable?' 24 ICSID Rev – FILJ 90

—2005. 'The Intervention of Private Entities and States as "Friends of the Court" in WTO Dispute Settlement Proceedings', in P F J Macrory, A E Appleton and M GPlummer (eds), *The World Trade Organization: Legal, Economic and Political Analysis* (New York: Springer), vol 1

—2002. 'L'entrée de la société civile dans l'arbitrage entre Etat et investisseur' 2 Revue de l'Arbitrage 329

Strong, S I 2013. *Class, Mass and Collective Arbitration in National and International Law* (Oxford University Press)

Szczudlik, K 2018. 'Effective Management of Mass Claims Arbitration: What We Could Learn from International Tribunals', in M Akbaba and G Capurro (eds), *International Challenges in Investment Arbitration* (New York: Routledge)

Toral, M and Schultz, T 2010. 'The State, a Perpetual Respondent in Investment Arbitration?', in M Waibel, A Kaushal, K-H Chung and C Balchin (eds), *The Backlash against Investment Arbitration: Perceptions and Reality* (London: Kluwer)

Treves, R T 2015. 'Equality of Arms and Inequality of Resources', in A Savarian, F Fontanelli, R Baker and V Tzevelekos (eds), *Procedural Fairness in International Courts and Tribunals* (London: British Institute of International and Comparative Law)

Ulmer, N 2010. 'The Cost Conundrum' 26 Arb Int'L 221

van Houtte, H and McAsey, B 2012. 'Case Comment, *Abaclat and Ors v Argentina*: ICSID, the BIT and Mass Claims' 27 ICSID Rev – FILJ 231

Vidal-Léon, C 2014. 'Inequality of the Parties before the International Court of Justice: Reflections on the Appellate Jurisdiction over ILOAT Judgments' 5 JIDS 406

Wälde, T 2010. 'Chapter 8: "Equality of Arms" in Investment Arbitration: Procedural Challenges', in K Yannaca-Small (ed), *Arbitration under International Investment Agreements: A Guide to the Key Issues* (Oxford University Press)

—2007. 'Introduction: International Investment Law Emerging from the Dynamics of Direct Investor–State Arbitration', in P Kahn and T Wälde (eds), *New Aspects of International Investment Law*, Hague Academy of International Law (Leiden and Boston, MA: Martinus Nijhoff)

Zimermann, A, Oellers-Frahm, K, Tomuschat, C and Tams, C J (eds) 2012. *The Statute of the International Court of Justice: A Commentary*, 2nd edn (Oxford University Press)

Reports

American Law Institute (ALI)/UNIDROIT 2004. *Principles of Transnational Civil Procedure* (Cambridge University Press)

European Commission (EC) 2015. 'Report: Online Public Consultation on Investment Protection and Investor-to-State Dispute Settlement (ISDS) in the Transatlantic Trade and Investment Partnership Agreement (TTIP)' (13 January), http://trade.ec.europa.eu/doclib/docs/2015/january/tradoc_153044.pdf

EC and Government of Canada 2017. 'The Case for Creating a Multilateral Investment Dispute Settlement Mechanism' (Informal ministerial meeting, World Economic Forum, Davos, 20 January)

European Union Council 2018. 'Negotiating Directives for a Convention Establishing a Multilateral Court for the Settlement of Investment Disputes' (20 March), 12981/17 ADD 1 DCL 1

France 2015. 'Towards a New Way to Settle Disputes between States and Investors' (May), www.diplomatie.gouv.fr

Geneva Center for International Dispute Settlement (CIDS) 2017. 'Supplemental Report: The Composition of a Multilateral Investment Court and of an Appeal Mechanism for Investment Awards' (15 November)

—(G Kaufmann-Kohler and M Potestà) 2016. 'Can the Mauritius Convention Serve as a Model for the Reform of Investor-State Arbitration in Connection with the Introduction of a Permanent Investment Tribunal or an Appeal Mechanism?'

Institut de Droit International 2013. 'Legal Aspects of Recourse to Arbitration by an Investor against the Authorities of the Host State under Inter-State Treaties' (Eighteenth Commission, A Giardina Rapporteur) 75 Annuaire 1, (2014) 29 ICSID Rev – FILJ 701

—2011. 'The Position of the International Judge' (Sixth Commission, G Guillaume Rapporteur) 74 Annuaire 3

—1989. 'Arbitration between States, State Enterprises, or State Entities and Foreign Enterprises' 63 Annuaire Pt I, 31–204 (preparatory work), Pt II, 121–2 (deliberations of the Institut), 324–31 (Resolution as adopted)

International Bar Association (IBA) 2014. 'IBA Guidelines on Conflicts of Interest in International Arbitration' (rev edn, adopted 23 October)

—2010. 'Commentary on the Revised Text of the 2010 IBA Rules on the Taking of Evidence in International Arbitration', www.ibanet.org/MediaHandler?id=DD240932-0E08-40D4-9866-309A635487C0

International Centre for the Settlement of Investment Disputes (ICSID) 2020a. 'Updated Backgrounder on Proposals for Amendment of the ICSID Rules' (28 February)

—2020b. 'Working Paper #4: Proposals for Amendment of the ICSID Rules' (28 February)

—2019a. 'Working Paper #2: Proposals for Amendment of the ICSID Rules' (March)

—2019b. 'Working Paper #3: Proposals for Amendment of the ICSID Rules' (August)

—2018a. 'Proposals for the Amendment of the ICSID Rules' (2 August)

—2018b. 'Schedule 8: Transparency – Access to Documents, Access to Hearings, and Non-Disputing Party Participating in ICSID Proceedings', in 'Working Paper #1: Proposals for Amendment of the ICSID Rules', vol 3 (2 August)

—2018c. 'Schedule 9: Addressing Time and Cost in ICSID Arbitration', in 'Working Paper #1: Proposals for Amendment of the ICSID Rules', vol 3 (2 August)

—1969. 'Documents Concerning the Origin and the Formulation of the Convention on the Settlement of Investment Disputes between States and Nationals of Other States'

—1965. 'Report of the Executive Directors on the Convention on the Settlement of Investment Disputes between States and Nationals of Other States'

ICSID Secretariat 2018. 'Working Paper #1: Proposals for Amendment of the ICSID Rules' (3 vols, 2 August)

ICSID/UN Commission on International Trade Law (UNCITRAL) 2020. 'Code of Conduct for Adjudicators in Investor–State Dispute Settlement' (1 May), https://uncitral.un.org/en/codeofconduct

International Chamber of Commerce (ICC) 2012. ICC Commission Report, 'States, State Entities and ICC Arbitration'

International Council for Commercial Arbitration (ICCA) 2018. 'Report of the ICCA-Queen Mary Task Force on Third-Party Funding in International Arbitration' (ICCA Report No 4, April)

International Law Association (ILA) 2005. Study Group on the Practice and Procedure of International Courts and Tribunals, 'Burgh House Principles on the Independence of the International Judiciary' (P Sands and C McLachlan, Co-Chairs) 4 LPICT 247

International Law Commission (ILC) 1955. 'Commentary on the Draft Convention on Arbitral Procedure Adopted by the International Law Commission at Its Fifth Session, Prepared by the Secretariat', UN Doc A/CN.4/92

NAFTA Free Trade Commission (FTC) 2004. 'Statement of the Free Trade Commission on Non-Disputing Party Participation', www.sice.oas.org/tpd/nafta/commission/nondispute_e.pdf

UNCITRAL 2020a. 'Report of Working Group III (Investor–State Dispute Settlement Reform) on the Work of Its Resumed Thirty-Eighth Session (Vienna, 20–24 January 2020)', UN Doc A/CN.9/1004/Add.1

—2020b. 'Selection and Appointment of ISDS Tribunal Members: Note by the Secretariat' (Draft working papers for comment), UN Doc A/CN.9/WG.III/WP

—2020c. 'Mulitple Proceedings and Counterclaims: Note by the Secretariat' (22 January), UN Doc A/CN.9/WG.III/WP.193

—2019a. 'Report of Working Group III (Investor–State Dispute Settlement Reform) on the Work of Its Thirty-Eighth Session (Vienna, 14–18 October 2019)', UN Doc A/CN.9/1004

—2019b. 'Background Information on a Code of Conduct: Note by the Secretariat' (31 July), UN Doc A/CN.9/WG.III/WP.167

—2019c. 'Advisory Centre: Note by the Secretariat' (25 July), UN Doc A/CN.9/WG.III/WP.168

—2019d. 'Third-Party Funding – Possible Solutions: Note by the Secretariat' (2 August), UN Doc A/CN.9/WG.III/WP.172

—2018. 'Report of Working Group III (Investor–State Dispute Settlement Reform) on the Work of Its Thirty-Fifth Session' (14 May), UN Doc A/CN.9/935

—2017a. 'Possible Future Work in the Field of Dispute Settlement: Reforms of Investor–State Dispute Settlement (ISDS) Note by the Secretariat' (20 April), UN Doc A/CN.9/917

—2017b. 'Note by the Secretariat: Working Group III (Investor–State Dispute Settlement Reform) Thirty-Fourth Session' (18 September), UN Doc A/CN.9/WG.III/WP.142

—2006. (J Paulson and G Petrochilos) 'Revision of the UNCITRAL Rules: A Report'

UN Conference on Trade and Development (UNCTAD) 2020. 'IIA Issues Note No 2' (July), UN Doc UNCTAD/DIAE/PCB/INF/2020/6

—2013. 'Reform of Investor–State Dispute Settlement: In Search of a Road-Map' (26 June)

UN Human Rights Committee (UNHRC) 2007. 'General Comment No 32 Article 14: Right to Equality before Courts and Tribunals and to a Fair Trial' (23 August), UN Doc CCPR/C/GC/32

UN Secretary-General 2012. 'Delivering Justice: Programme of Action to Strengthen the Rule of Law at the National and International Levels' (16 March), UN Doc A/66/749

World Trade Organization (WTO) 2017. 'Deepening Africa's Integration in the Global Economy through Trade and Investment Facilitation for Development: Abuja Statement' (7 November), Doc No WT/MIN(17)/4 WT/GC/186

INDEX